United States Government

by

Jane W. Smith
Carol Sullivan

AGS®
American Guidance Service
Circle Pines, Minnesota 55014-1796

The Authors

Jane Wilcox Smith received her Master of Arts in teaching as a reading specialist from Emory University in Atlanta, Georgia. She taught basic reading skills at the Schenck School in Atlanta. She now teaches remedial English and reading skills at Forsyth County High School.

Carol Sullivan received her Bachelor of Science degree from Jersey State College of New Jersey. She now teaches secondary Special Education at Forsyth County High School in Georgia and instructs students in the content areas, including social studies, science, and math.

Consultants

John L. Napp, M. S.
Social Studies Teacher (retired)
Talmudical Academy
Pikesville, Maryland

Wayne King, M. S.
Academic Dean
Baltimore School for the Arts
Baltimore, Maryland

Howard Berkowitz, M. A.
Social Studies Teacher
The Park School
Baltimore, Maryland

Printed in the United States of America
ISBN 0-88671-527-X
(Previously ISBN 0-7916-0091-2)
Order Number: 80310

A 0 9 8 7 6 5 4

Contents

Chapter 1

Chapter 2

Chapter 3

CONTENTS

CHIEF JUSTICE MARSHALL.

Chapter 13

CHAPTER ONE

Development of American Government

 All Groups of People Need Rules

WORDS TO KNOW

Ancient
Combination
Community
Complicated

Consider
Custom
Political

Many people live in large cities that are crowded and busy. Others make their homes far out in the country, where they can go for days without seeing another person. In between these two extremes are the people who live in towns and small *communities*. All of these people share a common need — the need for rules and laws to help them live peaceful and safe lives.

Every nation has a plan of action for running that country. Families have rules for their children; schools have rules for their students; and governments have rules for their citizens.

A government is a *combination* of laws and *customs* that people live by. Governments developed as the needs of people grew. Early groups of people lived simply, and simple rules were all they needed. They shared food, punished people who did wrong, and joined together for protection. As these groups grew into larger communities, life became more *complicated*. Governments grew in size and power in order to meet the needs of the new communities. As land and property became more important to people, rules were needed to protect these possessions.

How Did American Government Develop?

The government of America was formed because the early settlers, or colonists, did not like the way they were treated in England. The early American colonies belonged to England and were ruled by English law. Many things happened under these laws that upset the colonists. They were taxed unfairly and could not choose their own leaders. Soon the colonists decided to form their own government. They broke away from England.

The American colonists were careful to make rules and laws that were fair. The rights of people were also *considered* and written into the law. The colonists borrowed ideas from the past. All *political* ideas used by the colonists had their roots in older forms of government. *Ancient* civilizations such as Greece and Rome had an influence. The greatest influence, however, came from the governments in England and Europe at that time.

★**Activity A:** Number your paper from 1 to 5. Use the words from the list below to complete each sentence. Copy the complete sentences onto your paper.

ancient   *considered*
combination   *customs*
complicated   *political*
community

1. People in a ___ need rules and laws to live peaceful lives.
2. A government is a ___ of laws and ___.
3. Governments grew in size and power when life became more ___.
4. The colonists ___ the rights of the people when they made rules and laws.
5. Many ___ ideas used by the colonists had their roots in ___ governments.

PART 2 ★ ★ ★ Influence of Ancient Governments

W O R D S   T O   K N O W
Appoint   *Dictator*
Democratic   *Revolt*

The word "democracy," which comes from the Greek language, means "rule by the people." The idea of a *democratic* government began in Greece in 600 B.C., about twenty-five hundred years ago. Greece was made up of city-states. These were cities with large amounts of land around them. In the beginning these city-states were ruled by kings, and then they were ruled by landowners. Some were even ruled by *dictators*. Dictators can rule any way that they please, no matter what the people want. Some dictators became unpopular with the people. The people *revolted* against them. The people wanted to govern themselves, so they formed democracies.

This "rule by the people," or democratic rule, did not mean that all people could take part in running the city-states. The people were divided into groups. There were free men, women, young males, and slaves. Only free men were members of the ruling body, called an Assembly. All the free males ran the government and took turns holding office. The Greek city-state, Athens, had the best-run government.

The city-states of Greece were always at war with one another, and they became weak. Rome, another great power, soon took over the weakened Greek city-states.

Ancient Rome Had a Representative Form of Government

Because Rome had such a large population, all of the free males could not take part in running the government. The citizens elected people to speak and act for them. The people they chose were their representatives. This representative type of government was called a republic. Rome was a republic.

Rome, like Greece, did not give slaves, women, or young males a part in running the government. The free men who ran the government were divided into two groups. The wealthy, or rich, males had greater power and were called patricians. The common people, or workers, were called the plebeians. From the patricians, two consuls, or leaders, were chosen. These consuls in turn *appointed* senators, also from the wealthy class. Senators were appointed for life, and the Senate was the most powerful part of the government. The Senate made rules and laws, which could be vetoed (veto means "I forbid") by the common people, or plebeians. Rome's government changed several times during its history, but remained a republic for quite a while. When the Roman Empire came to an end, it was being ruled by dictators and emperors, who were like kings.

The United States borrowed many ideas from these ancient civilizations. The country has a representative form of government with elected representatives who make laws and rules. Words such as Senate, veto, republic, representative, and democracy are used to descibe the government process and are used in official documents.

★**Activity B:** Number your paper from 1 to 10. Decide if each statement below tells about the Roman government or the Greek government. Write *Greece* or *Rome* after each number.

1. Its representative form of government was known as a republic.
2. The common people were called plebeians.
3. The country was made up of city-states.
4. The ruling body was called an Assembly.
5. All free males took turns holding office.
6. Senators were appointed for life.
7. Consuls, or leaders, were chosen from the wealthy class.
8. The wealthy, or rich, citizens were called patricians.
9. The city-states of this country were always at war.
10. Democracy, or "rule by the people," began with this government.

PART 3 ★ ★ ★ The Influence of English History

WORDS TO KNOW

Decision   *Legislature*
Generation   *Petition*
Jury   *Similar*
Lawsuit

Some early forms of government did not have rule by the people. They were far from being democracies. Three common forms of government were the monarchy, the dictatorship, and the oligarchy.

In a monarchy, the country is ruled by one family, *generation* after generation. The leadership is passed down to the eldest son or daughter. The rulers have titles like king, queen, empress, or emperor. A dictator rules alone in a dictatorship. He does not pass the rule down to the next generation. No limit is placed on how long a dictator can rule. In an oligarchy, the rule is in the hands of a few people. These rulers may be from a military group or from a group given special training by its government.

Rule of Henry II

During the late 1000s and early 1100s, the government of England changed form many times. The constant changing of power had kept the country in a state of confusion. The rights of the common person had not been considered. In 1154 Henry II became king. He was a strong monarch who made changes in the government that did consider the rights of the common person.

Henry II appointed judges and gave them authority. These judges traveled throughout the country to hold court. They decided how to punish people who disobeyed the law. Soon all these decisions about offenses and their punishments

Henry II was a twelfth century monarch who considered the rights of the common person when he made changes in the government.

became rules and were followed as law. These laws were divided into two types. The first type, criminal law, included rules that everyone must obey. The second type, private law, had to do with rights and duties between individuals. For instance, if a person borrowed money and did not pay it back, he could face a *lawsuit*.

Words such as plaintiff (the person offended) and defendant (the person who is accused of committing the offense) are words we use today that came from the English private system of law.

Our *jury* system was also influenced by this law under Henry II. As the judges traveled from place to place, they were told of all the crimes committed in an area. Henry II had appointed special people to inform the judges. Today we have a grand jury system with duties *similar* to this. They tell our officials if there has been a crime committed and if it should come to trial. If a person in our system is accused of a crime he comes before the grand jury first.

Our trial-by-jury system is also similar to the system Henry II used. Twelve local citizens were asked by the traveling judges to swear under oath whether or not they thought the plaintiff's statements were true. The *decision* of these twelve citizens helped the judge decide on the punishment for the crime. The jury decides if a person is guilty or not guilty. The judge then decides on the punishment, in most cases.

The Parliament

Parliament is the name of the lawmaking body in England. In very early times only the king and his lords could make laws. Then in the 1200s, common people were allowed to elect representatives to take part in the meetings. The common people were merchants or property owners. By 1400 Parliament had two parts: the House of Lords, which included nobles and church leaders, and the House of Commons, which included knights and common people.

Parliament was used by some rulers and ignored by others. Finally the Parliament was allowed to make laws on its own. The system that Parliament used to make laws worked very well. The colonists followed the same system. It is the idea behind our Congress and state *legislatures*.

The Petition of Right and the English Bill of Rights

The "*Petition* of Right" was drawn up by the English Parliament in 1628 to put a limit on the power a king could have. The kings, or monarchs, always claimed they were given their power by God. This idea was known as the "divine right of kings." By 1628 the members of Parliament felt that the power of the kings had become too strong. In the Petition of Right they listed the things that a king could not do. It said, among other things, that a king could not force rich people to make loans or put people in prison without a jury trial.

Parliament did not always remain strong. Some kings ignored Parliament. During the reign of William and Mary, in 1689, Parliament again gained power and passed the English Bill of Rights. This gave many rights back to the people. It stated the powers that a king or queen had. Under this Bill of Rights, Parliament had to approve all taxes. The king was not allowed to suspend, or stop, the work of Parliament. The people could ask the government for help, and a person accused of a crime had the right to a jury trial.

The settlers who came to America knew about the rights that were included in the English Bill of Rights. When these settlers saw that England was trying to take away some of their rights, they revolted, and a war was fought. The settlers declared their independence from English rule, and a new country was born. When the citizens of this new country wrote a plan for their own government, they also added a Bill of Rights, using what they knew from the English Bill of Rights and the Petition of Right. In Chapter 3 you will study the freedoms listed in the Bill of Rights.

★Activity C: Number your paper from 1 to 5 and write the answers to these questions.

1. Which form of government has a ruler who does not have to pass the rule to the next generation?

2. What system of justice that we use today was based on a system used during the reign of Henry II?

3. Parliament is made up of the House of Lords and which other house?

4. What part of our government today is based on the English Parliament?

5. Name one English document that influenced the American settlers when they wrote the Bill of Rights.

THE MAGNA CARTA

The king of England in 1199 was King John. This king was unfair and made many enemies. For one thing he taxed the people very heavily. The people did not want to pay all the taxes. They believed that the king was spending the money on himself.

The nobles (rich people of the country) decided that something must be done to check the king. They planned very carefully. Together with town leaders and church officials, they presented King John with a petition known as the Magna Carta. In June of 1215, King John finally agreed to the demands and put his seal on the paper.

This charter gave certain rights to the English people and limited the king's power. It stated that the king must ask advice of the nobles in important matters. It also said that no special taxes could be raised without the nobles' consent. No free man could be put in prison except after being judged by his peers (equals). Judges and other officials were to be appointed to serve the kingdom.

The important ideas written in the Magna Carta were then used by

HIGHLIGHT
STORY
★ ★ ★

many people for hundreds of years. For example, one complaint the American colonists had against England was that they were being taxed without their consent and that they had "taxation without representation." The practice of trial by jury developed from the Magna Carta. This charter helped rulers recognize the wants, needs, and rights of the common people.

Review

Answer the following questions in complete sentences.

1. Which three groups of people developed the petition that became known as the Magna Carta?
2. Why did they send the petition to King John?
3. The Magna Carta was agreed upon and signed by King John. Explain one way the power of the King was limited by the Magna Carta.
4. Name one important practice that still exists in today's government that developed from ideas written in the Magna Carta.
5. Why do you think the Magna Carta is conisdered an important document?

PART 4 ★★★ Ideas From Thirteen Original Colonies

WORDS TO KNOW

Contract
Criticize
Loyal
National

Press
Publication
Strict

The early settlers in America had ideas about forming a new government. One group of settlers, the Pilgrims, left England because they did not want to belong to the Church of England or pay taxes. Before they left their ship, they wrote a *contract* for all to sign. This contract, called the Mayflower Compact, said that these settlers would write fair laws and choose leaders. They would do these things but remain *loyal* to the king. As their colony in Massachusetts grew, each church became a meeting place, and each person had a vote. These Pilgrims had the first ideas about democracy (rule by the people) in America. Other political ideas soon followed.

In other colonies people did not all vote as they did in the Pilgrim colony. The Jamestown colony was the first to have an assembly of representatives. This assembly, called the House of Burgesses, made decisions for the people. The people elected the representatives. The plan for the assembly did not come from the settlers, but was set up by England. England also sent a governor to rule.

The ideas of voting and electing representatives that began in these colonies were later used in modern American government. Today we elect representatives at all levels of government: city, county, state, and *national*.

The first ideas of democracy in America came from the pilgrims who, while still aboard the Mayflower, wrote a contract saying that they would write fair laws and choose leaders.

The First Constitution in America Was Written in Connecticut in 1639

#2 Some of the people who were living in Massachusetts decided that the Puritan rule there was too *strict for them.* They moved away and settled in the Connecticut area. The leader of this group was Thomas #3 Hooker. Hooker believed in a more democratic government that would give more control to the people.

Hooker and his followers drew up a constitution. A constitution is a written plan for government. It lists the powers of the government, as well as the rights of the people. In its constitution, the Connecticut group agreed to create an assembly with elected representatives. The group agreed to elect a governor and judges.

This first constitution set an example. Soon other colonies were writing constitutions of their own. Massachusetts even set up a public school system which was paid for with tax money.

Years later, in 1787, the writers of the United States Constitution took many ideas from these early colonial constitutions.

The Idea of a Free Press

In colonial times there was a law in the New York area that said that no one could publish anything that

Public Schools Began in Massachusetts

In the early colonial days, children were educated at home or in private schools. Only the wealthy colonists were able to send their children to private schools. Children of poor parents were required to work at an early age. In 1647 this policy of education began to change when the colony of Massachusetts passed a law establishing public schools. All towns of fifty or more people were told to set up a school and hire a school teacher. The money for the school came from the town's tax money. The Puritans of this colony felt that all children should learn to read the Bible in order to avoid evil ways. Even though these first schools were set up for religious reasons, it was an important step in the country towards free public education. The responsibility for education was shifted from the home to the community.

Other colonies were slow to follow the example set by Massachusetts. It was not until the early 1800s that a system of free public education was widespread throughout the country. Even then, children were only educated through elementary school. Only after the Civil War was a system of high schools set up in many states.

spoke out against the government. A newspaper reporter, John Peter Zenger, wrote an article that sharply criticized the governor. He was tried for breaking the law. The jury, however, decided against the law and said that Zenger was innocent. This was a big step toward the idea of a free *press* as we know it. It is not against the law to *criticize* the government or its leaders in a newspaper or other *publication*.

The Idea of Religious Freedom

Many colonists came to America to worship as they pleased. The Puritans came for this reason, but they would not give religious freedom to people living in their colony. People who disagreed with the Puritans were sent away, or left the Puritan colony.

These people then set up colonies that did allow a few different religions. This idea of religious freedom soon spread throughout the colonies. It finally led to our system today, which guarantees people the right to worship as they please.

★**Activity D:** Number your paper from 1 to 10. Write the answer next to the number.

1. Which colony of early settlers had the first group of elected representatives?
2. Which of the early colonies had a very strict rule?
3. Who set up a colony with a more democratic rule than the Puritan colony?
4. What is a written plan for government called?
5. What officers did the Connecticut group decide to elect?
6. Which colony set up the first public school system?
7. Who wrote a newspaper article that criticized the governor?
8. What did the jury decide about John Peter Zenger?
9. What freedom permits people to publish critical remarks about the government?
10. What freedom permits people to worship freely?

American Colonies Join Together

WORDS TO KNOW
Allegiance   *Interfere*
Commerce

England did not *interfere* with the government in the colonies for nearly a century. Then the English needed money to pay their debts. They tried to raise money from the colonies. By the middle 1700s, the colonists felt that England was trying to regain control. The colonists did not like the high taxes or the duties collected on certain goods. England passed the Stamp Act, which forced the colonists to pay a tax on all newspapers, pamphlets, legal documents, calendars, and playing cards. In order to end this taxation, representatives from the colonies met together in 1765. Other meetings followed. Gradually feelings against the English rule increased.

The First Continental Congress

In 1774 a large meeting called the First Continental Congress was held in Philadelphia. At this meeting the colonists decided to take action against England. They sent the king of England a list of the rights they demanded. They also said that they

Representatives from the colonies formed the First Continental Congress to take action against England by sending a list of the rights they demanded and by refusing to buy all British goods.

were refusing to buy all British goods, including tea.

This action of the First Continental Congress made no difference in the way England treated the colonists. Trouble continued between the colonists and England. The English soldiers (Redcoats) and the colonial soldiers (Minutemen) began shooting on April 19, 1775. The Revolutionary War was underway.

The Second Continental Congress

This Second Continental Congress met a few weeks after the shooting began. They organized an army led by George Washington. The colonists were ready to fight the British. The Second Continental Congress ran the government of the colonies and supported the colonists' cause during the war.

Soon the Continental Congress realized that the trouble with England would not end peacefully, but they wanted to end British rule once and for all. They also wanted to have a government run by the people — a democracy. They asked Thomas Jefferson to write down all their ideas to send to the king. This document was called the Declaration of Independence. It was the greatest contribution of the colonial period to the future form of democratic government in America.

The Declaration of Independence Told England That the Colonists Were Ending English Rule

The first part of the Declaration of Independence states that all people have certain rights, including "life, liberty, and the pursuit of happiness." It goes on to say that if a government denies these rights to the people, then that rule must end.

The middle section of the Declaration lists all the grievances, or complaints, the colonists had against the king of England, George III. The Declaration ends with an explanation of what the colonists have done to change the attitude of the English, but says that the English have been "deaf to the voice of justice..."

The very last paragraph of the Declaration says, in part:

"...That these united colonies are, and of right ought to be, free and independent States; that they are absolved from all allegiance to the British Crown, and that all political connection between them and the state of Great Britain, is and ought to be totally dissolved; and that as free and

independent states, they have full power to levy war, conclude peace, contract alliances, establish commerce, and to do all other acts and things which independent states may of right do...."

★**Activity E:** Number your paper from 1 to 7. Choose the correct phrase to complete each sentence. Write the letter of that phrase next to the number.

1. By the middle 1700s the colonists felt that England was
   (a) trying to regain control.
   (b) treating the colonists fairly.
2. The Stamp Act
   (a) helped the colonies.
   (b) forced the colonists to pay unfair taxes.
3. At the First Continental Congress, the colonists
   (a) decided to take action against England.
   (b) organized an army to fight the British.
4. The colonists sent England a list of the rights they demanded and said that they
   (a) would not buy British goods.
   (b) wanted to fight a war.
5. The group that ran the government of the country during the war between the colonists and the English was the
   (a) First Continental Congress.
   (b) Second Continental Congress.
6. The Declaration of Independence, which told England that the colonies were independent, was written by
   (a) Thomas Jefferson.
   (b) the Second Continental Congress.
7. The Declaration of Independence broke all ties with England and
   (a) listed the grievances the colonists had against the king.
   (b) wrote a new plan of government for the colonies.

C H A P T E R ★ S U M M A R Y

Government came into existence as the needs of people changed. American government began when the colonists realized they no longer wanted to live under British rule. They had to form their own government. Ancient governments, as well as the English government, influenced the development of democratic government in America.

Ideas from the ancient governments of Greece and Rome were used by the American colonists when they formed their own government. In Greece, male citizens had a say in government; Rome had a senate and senators that voted for laws. The Senate in the United States works in much the same way.

King Henry II of England, a strong ruler, considered the rights of the common man. He appointed judges and used a jury system. The trial-by-jury system used today in the United States had its beginnings in the system used by Henry II.

Another strong influence on American government was the English Parliament. It had some elected officials who made the laws. Parliament was the basis for the American Congress and the individual state legislatures.

Political ideas for American government also came from the original thirteen colonies. Some of these ideas are found in the Mayflower Compact and in Connecticut's constitution. The ideas of free press and freedom of religion also began in the colonies. Today freedom of the press and the freedom to worship as you please are basic American rights.

C H A P T E R ★ R E V I E W

Comprehension:
Identification
Directions: Number your paper from 1 to 10. Choose the correct word or words from the list to match each statement. Write the answers on a separate sheet of paper.

democracy   John Peter Zenger
Jamestown   Magna Carta
Henry II   Monarchy
senate   Mayflower Compact
Declaration of Independence
Second Continental Congress

1. This Greek word means "rule by the people." _____
2. This group in ancient Rome made the rules and laws. _____
3. In this type of government the rulers have titles like King, Queen, or Emperor. _____
4. King John agreed to the demands written into this document. _____
5. When this king came into power (1154), he considered the rights of the common people. _____
6. This important document was written by the Pilgrims before they left the Mayflower. _____
7. This early colony had an elected assembly called the House of Burgesses. _____
8. This man wrote a newspaper article criticizing the governor. _____
9. This group ran the government of the colonies during the Revolutionary War. _____
10. This important document, written by Thomas Jefferson, stated that the colonies were now "free and independent." _____

Comprehension:
Understanding Main Ideas
Directions: Write the answers to the following questions using complete sentences.

1. In the beginning, the American colonies belonged to England. Give two reasons why the colonists broke away from England.
2. What two ancient civilizations had a great influence on the development of American government?
3. What important system in today's American government is based on ideas used by Henry II of England?
4. The Bill of Rights was added to the American plan of government and was based on some ideas in the English Bill of Rights. Name three of these ideas taken from the English Bill of Rights.
5. After the Revolutionary War began, the colonists sent the English King a document. What was this document called? Why did the colonists feel English rule of the colonies should end?

Critical Thinking:
Write Your Opinion
1. Which idea from English government do you think had the greatest influence on American government?
2. Why do you think England did not want to give up the American colonies and was even willing to go to war to keep them?

CHAPTER TWO

★ ★ ★

Creation of American Government

PART 1
★ ★ ★
Joining the Colonies Together

W O R D S   T O   K N O W

Delegate   *Limited*
Financial   *Revise*
Justice   *Treaty*

In the last chapter you learned that the Declaration of Independence broke all ties the colonies had with England. A new nation was formed, but it was a nation of separate and individual colonies. These colonies needed a form of government to join them together as a country.

At the Second Continental Congress a committee was working to write a plan for a government that would join the states together. This plan was called the Articles of Confederation.

Because of the great need, the Articles were quickly approved by all the states. It gave the thirteen states a plan for government. It was popular with the states because it did not make the national, or central, government too strong. The colonists remembered their dislike for the strong English rule.

The Articles of Confederation gave the government a national Congress made up of *delegates* from the thirteen states. This Congress could make war, agree to *treaties* with other countries, and take care of *financial* needs. Each state sent one delegate to the Congress. The Articles did not provide for a president as a national leader, or for a system of *justice*.

At first most people were satisfied with the Articles becuase they allowed the states control over most of their own affairs. The Articles *limited* Congress's power over the states. However, as time went on, the states saw that the Articles were too weak. The war that set the colonies free cost a great deal of money. The country owed 40 million dollars to foreign governments alone. Congress had no money of its own, and no way of raising money. Most of the money needed should have come from the states, but many states refused to pay. There was no system of law to force the states to pay. In addition the Articles of Confederation did not provide for a system of law or justice.

Other financial problems, besides the war debt, were also facing the new nation. Businesses and farmers were out of money. Congress had no funds to pay an army and navy to defend the nation. Also, the soldiers who fought in the Revolutionary War had not yet been paid. Individual states were printing their own money. Something had to be done. A better government had to be worked out if the United States of America was to be a strong, rich country. Finally, a meeting was called to *revise* the Articles of Confederation. This meeting was held in Philadelphia in 1787, and became known as the Constitutional Convention.

★**Activity A:** Number your paper from 1 to 5. Choose the correct word or words in parentheses that make each statement true. Write your answer next to each number.

1. The Declaration of Independence (broke, began) all ties the colonies had with England.

2. At first the Articles of Confederation were (unpopular, popular) with the people in the colonies because the Articles joined them together as a country.

3. The Articles of Confederation (did, did not) make the central, or national, government strong.

4. The Articles of Confederation (did, did not) provide for a president of the new country.

5. Congress (had, did not have) money to pay for an army and navy to defend the nation.

PART 2 ★★★ The Constitutional Convention

WORDS TO KNOW

Executive   *Legislature*
Federal   *Safeguards*

The delegates who attended the Constitutional Convention were well-educated men, mostly from the cities. They shared the same ideas about government, and were important people in their own states. George Washington was the leader at the convention. At first the delegates worked to revise the Articles of Confederation, but soon they saw that a new plan for government would be necessary.

The colonists knew what they did not want. They did not want the states to lose control of the government. They did not want a king or a strong central government. Although the Articles of Confederation had provided these *safeguards*, that plan had failed. The delegates worked for four months in secret to create a new plan for the country. This new plan for a national government was the Constitution.

A *federal* government is one in which states join together to form a country. Some, but not all, power is given to a central government. The states are equal to each other in voting power, and are also given some responsibility to govern themselves. This federal type of government that the convention delegates finally worked out was the answer to the new nation's problems.

Several forms of federal government were suggested at first.

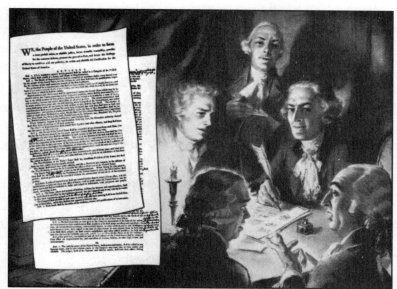

The members of the Constitutional Convention had the job of planning a new form of government for the United States. It took them four months of debating in secrecy to finally agree on a plan.

The delegates looked at all of the suggestions. Two plans were finally presented for discussion:

Virginia Plan. The Virginia Plan, suggested by the larger states, favored a strong central government. It called for one *executive*, and a two-part lawmaking body (*legislature*). The people would elect members of the legislature.

New Jersey Plan. The New Jersey Plan, suggested by the smaller states, favored greater power for the states. It offered a one-part legislature and two or more executives. All members of the legislature would be chosen by the states. The presidents would be chosen by the legislature.

Both plans provided for the federal government to be in charge of admitting new states to the union. Both plans favored a supreme court that would make final decisions concerning the law.

★Activity B: Number your paper from 1 to 7. Match the definitions in Part 1 with the terms in Part 2. Write the correct term by each number.

Part 1, Definitions:
1. Leader of the delegates at the Constitutional Convention.
2. Meeting held to revise the Articles of Confederation.
3. The people who attended the Constitutional Convention.
4. First plan of government that failed.
5. Plan that favored a strong central government.
6. Type of government which does not give all power to a national, or central, government.
7. Plan that favored greater power to the states.

Part 2, Terms:
Federal government
George Washington
Delegates
Constitutional Convention
Articles of Confederation
Virginia Plan
New Jersey Plan

CONSTITUTIONAL CONVENTION WAS HELD IN SECRET

The Constitutional Convention began in the early summer of 1787. The doors to Philadelphia's State House, later known as Independence Hall, where the Constitutional Convention was held, were always guarded. Only the official delegates to the Convention were allowed inside. Each delegate at the Convention had agreed ahead of time not to discuss Convention business with outsiders.

Why all the secrecy at the convention? The delegates, being very learned men, understood the problems the country faced. They knew the decisions facing them were going to be difficult. The delegates wanted to settle their differences of opinion and form their proposals for a new government in private. Only then would the public be allowed to judge their proposals.

Although official records of the Convention's proceedings were kept, James Madison kept his own notes. The notes were kept secret until after his death in 1836. According to his notes, we know much about the convention. Although the delegates represented different sections of the country with different interests, they did agree on the following issues: the Articles of Confederation could not be revised, the country needed a strong central government, the power of the government must rest in the voters who would elect men to run the government for them and the power of government needed to be separated. They also knew that the new government must be able to tax, raise an army, and regulate commerce.

Finally, as the summer was ending, the hard work of the Convention ended. Many compromises had been made to settle the differences and now the delegates had a plan to present to the states for their approval. All that remained was for the states to ratify the document. This also proved to be a difficult struggle.

Review

On your own paper, answer the following questions using complete sentences.

1. Where was the Constitutional Convention held?
2. Why did the delegates meet in secret?
3. Name two issues concerning the new government which all of the delegates agreed upon.
4. Who took complete notes at the Convention?
5. After the Convention was concluded, what did the delegates do with the new plan for government?

PART 3 **Compromises Made**
★ ★ ★ **at the Convention**

W O R D S   T O   K N O W
Compromise

Compromising is a system of give and take used by opposing sides when an agreement cannot be reached. At the Convention, each side had to *compromise*, or give up, some of its plan in order to reach an agreement. The people who favored the Virginia Plan, and those who favored the New Jersey plan, worked out their differences. Four major compromises were made:

Compromise One

The most important compromise was made by a group of delegates from Connecticut. It dealt with the problem of creating a legislature (lawmaking body) for the new government. These delegates said it should be a two-part legislature in order to please both the larger and smaller states. The members of one part would be chosen according to population. The other part would have two representatives from each state, no matter how small.

Compromise Two

The second compromise settled a problem about slaves. The problem was whether the slaves should be counted the same as free men for tax collection and population purposes. The compromise said that every five slaves would count the same as three free men. This was called the Three-Fifths Compromise. Both the North and South accepted this plan.

Compromise Three

The third compromise had to do with commerce (trade). Everyone agreed that the states should control trade within their own borders. A question that remained was who would control foreign trade and trade among the states.

Compromise Four

Northerners wanted the new national government to have full power. The Southerners feared that the government might end slave trade. The fourth compromise gave the federal government power over foreign trade and trade among the states. It also said that slave trade could not be ended by the federal government for 20 years, or until 1808. This satisfied the Southern states.

By September 17, 1787, the compromises were agreed upon by all the delegates, and the Constitution was signed. The country had a new plan for government. The Constitution of the United States was, and still is, the foundation of the country's law.

★Activity C: Number your paper from 1 to 5. Select the correct ending for each sentence.
1. A compromise is a system
   (a) of give and take by each side in a disagreement.
   (b) of rules and laws to run a country.
2. The delegates from Connecticut tried to settle the problems about
   (a) a legislature.
   (b) the slaves.
3. Everyone at the Convention agreed that the states should control
   (a) their own trade.
   (b) all foreign trade.
4. One compromise that the delegates agreed on was that slave trade could
   (a) never be ended.
   (b) not be ended by the federal government for twenty years.
5. On September 17, 1787, the compromises were agreed upon by
   (a) all delegates.
   (b) only some of the delegates.

PART 4 ★ ★ ★ Guiding Principles of the Constitution

WORDS TO KNOW

Balances
Executive
Judicial

Principles
Separation

The writers of the Constitution were careful to base this new plan on certain *principles* they felt were necessary for a democratic government. These principles are Popular Sovereignty, Limited Government, *Separation* of Powers, and Checks and *Balances*.

Popular Sovereignty

Popular Sovereignty is when all power is held by the people because they elect the leaders of the national and state governments.

Limited Government

The Constitution set limits on the power the government has. Government must obey the law and conduct business according to the principles of the Constitution. The government and its officers are never above the law.

Separation of Powers

The Constitution put the power into three different departments — the Congress, which is the legislative

Limits of the Branches of Government

Presidential Limits

1. Congress can remove the president by impeachment.
2. Congress can pass a bill even if the president vetoes it.
3. Congress must approve how money is spent.
4. Only Congress can declare war.

Congressional Limits

1. President can veto bills of Congress.
2. Supreme Court can say a law is unfair.

Judicial Limits

1. President decides on all federal judges.
2. Congress must approve president's appointments of judges.
3. Congress can remove a judge.

Laws can never be made by the Supreme Court, but the court can decide if a law is unfair. The Congress then has to change the law or write a new law. The President cannot make laws on his own, but approves the laws Congress passes. In turn the Congress must approve all money spent by the country. Congress must also approve presidential appointments of people to important government jobs.

or lawmaking branch; the *executive* branch, which applies or enforces the laws; and the *judicial* branch, which interprets the laws made by Congress.

Congress alone can make laws. It cannot give anyone else the power to do so. It also must approve appointments made by the president. The president and the executive branch see that the laws are carried out. The president can also veto bills and appoint officials, such as ambassadors and judges.

The courts, with the Supreme Court as the most powerful court, can settle disagreements or disputes brought to them by the government or by private persons. The judicial branch interprets the laws (tells what they mean). It can tell whether or not the law follows the Constitution.

Checks and Balances

The three branches of government have separate duties, but they must act together in some cases. This balances the power and never allows one branch to become too powerful. Limits are placed on each branch.

★**Activity D:** Which basic principle of the Constitution is described in each statement below? Number your paper from 1 to 4. Write the correct principle by the number.

limited government
popular sovereignty
checks and balances
separation of powers

1. The power of the federal government is held by three groups: Congress, the president, and a system of courts.
2. The three branches of the government work together and also check on each other.
3. The government and its officers are never above the law. They cannot take away the rights of the people as guaranteed in the Constitution.
4. The people elect the leaders of the federal (central) and state governments.

PART 5 ★ ★ ★ The Struggle for Approval

W O R D S   T O   K N O W
Authority   *Persuade*
Essays

After all work on the Constitution was complete, it had to be approved by the states. Most of the delegates at the Convention had signed the Constitution. These delegates worked hard to *persuade* the states to ratify (approve) it. Each state held a convention to study the Constitution. The approval of nine of the thirteen states was needed before the Constitution could be put into use.

It had been eleven years since the Declaration of Independence was signed. The people of the country were divided in their ideas about the Constitution. Some people favored the Constitution because it provided for a strong national government. These people were known as Federalists. The Federalists believed a strong central *authority* was necessary to defend the nation and keep it united. Alexander Hamilton strongly favored the Constitution and wrote *essays* in the newspapers to persuade people to vote for it. Another group, known as the Anti-Federalists, were opposed to the Constitution.

They were mostly wealthy business people. They favored stronger state governments than the Constitution permitted. These people were afraid that a strong central, or national, government would take away some of their rights.

The Anti-Federalists were against the Constitution because they were afraid of losing individual rights. When a change giving people basic rights was suggested for the Constitution, many Anti-Federalists then favored it. This addition was made two years later and was known as the Bill of Rights. It guaranteed such rights as freedom of speech, religion, and of the press.

Discussions continued throughout the winter at the state conventions. Finally, by June of 1788, nine states had ratified the Constitution — enough to allow the Constitution to become the new plan for government. By 1790 all thirteen states had ratified the Constitution.

The New Nations Under the Constitution

Congress began putting the Constitution into use as soon as it was ratified. The first action Congress took was to name New York as the temporary capital. Later it was moved to Philadelphia, and by 1800, to Washington, D.C., the present capital. The first elections were held, and George Washington was the popular choice for president. John Adams was elected vice president. Twenty-two senators and fifty-nine representatives were elected from the states to serve in the new Congress. They met for the first time on March 4, 1789, in Federal Hall in New York.

The dome of the Capitol building, located in Washington, D. C., is a symbol of the United States government.

★**Activity E:** Number your paper from 1 to 5. Choose the correct answer from the three choices given that best completes the sentences. Write this answer by the number.

1. The (Anti-Federalists, Federalists, Congress) favored the new Constitution.
2. The Federalists favored a (strong, weak, complete) national government.
3. The Constitution had to be approved by (eight, nine, ten) of the thirteen states in order to be ratified.
4. The (Anti-Federalists, Federalists, Constitution) favored strong state governments.
5. Finally, by 1790, (all, some, ten) of the thirteen states had ratified the Constitution.

C H A P T E R ★ S U M M A R Y

The colonists finally broke all ties with England when the Declaration of Independence was approved. The next step was to write a plan for the government that would join the thirteen separate states together as a country. While the Declaration was still being written, another group of people began writing a plan for running the government of the new country.

This first plan to unite the states into a country was called the Articles of Confederation. It provided for a Congress made up of representatives from all the states. The Articles were quickly accepted by the states, but soon the weaknesses of the Articles were seen. Under the Articles of Confederation, the government did not have the power to raise money needed to pay the nation's war debt, or to force the states to pay their share of the debt.

Another meeting, known as the Constitutional Convention, was called to revise the Articles of Confederation. The delegates at this convention decided that a new, stronger plan for government was necessary. Although a federal form of government was agreed upon, all of the delegates did not agree on how the government would be run. The larger states favored a strong central government (Virginia Plan), while the smaller states wanted more power to go to the states (New Jersey Plan). After long discussions and several compromises, the new Constitution became the plan for government.

The Constitution was written based on certain principles, or ideals. These principles are Popular Sovereignty, Limited Government, Separation of Powers, and Checks and Balances.

After the Constitution was finished it had to be approved, or ratified, by the states. Each state held a convention. The Federalists, who favored a stronger central government, approved of the Constitution. They were opposed by the Anti-Federalists, who said the states should have more power. The Anti-Federalists felt the Constitution would take away their individual rights. Some people suggested that a Bill of Rights be added to the Constitution to guarantee people's rights. When the Bill of Rights was suggested, many Anti-Federalists changed their minds and voted for the Constitution. After almost a year of discussions at the state conventions, nine states ratified the Constitution, and it became the new plan for government. New York was chosen as the temporary capital, and George Washington was elected president. Soon every state in the country had ratified the Constitution, and the new, independent nation was established.

C H A P T E R ★ R E V I E W

Comprehension:
Identification
Directions: Number your paper from 1 to 10. Next to each number, write the word or phrase that is missing.

compromises   Nine
three   smaller
right away   federal
national leader
first plan of government
Declaration of Independence
Popular sovereignty

1. The ___ was written by the colonists to break all ties with England.
2. The Articles of Confederation were written as the ___ for the new country.
3. The Articles of Confederation did not provide for a ___ or a system of law or justice.
4. In a ___ form of government, some power is given to a central government, and some power is given to the states.
5. The ___ states at the Constitutional Convention favored more power for the individual states.
6. Many ___ were made at the Constitutional Convention before the delegates approved the Constitution.
7. ___ means that power is in the hands of the people because they elect the leaders.
8. The separation of powers among the ___ branches of the government was provided for by the Constitution.

9. ___ of the thirteen states had to ratify, or approve, the Constitution before it could be used.
10. When the Constitution was ratified, it was put into use ___.

Comprehension:
Understanding Main Ideas
Directions: Write the answers to the following questions using complete sentences.

1. Why were the Articles of Confederation accepted at first by all the states as a plan for the new government?
2. Name one reason the Articles of Confederation were considered to be too weak to run the country.
3. The colonists met in Philadelphia to draw up the new plan for government. Explain the type of government they finally agreed on.
4. When the new Constitution was finally agreed upon, what type of legislature was chosen?
5. In writing the Constitution, what were the four guiding principles considered?

Critical Thinking:
Write Your Opinion

1. In writing the Constitution the New Jersey plan was rejected by the delegates at the convention. Why do you think the delegates rejected this plan?
2. Of the four guiding principles followed when the Constitution was written, which do you consider to be the most important and why?

CHAPTER THREE

★ ★ ★

A Look at the Constitution

Preamble and First Four Articles

WORDS TO KNOW

Articles   *Preamble*

Justice   *Vested*

The Constitution, written in Philadelphia and approved by the states, became the new plan for government for the United States of America. It contained a *preamble*, or introduction, and seven *articles* that explained how the new government should be set up and run. Amendments, or written changes, were added to the Constitution as they were needed. The first ten amendments, known as the Bill of Rights, were added just two years after the Constitution was ratified.

The Constitution has been in use for over two hundred years. It has remained strong even though the country has changed from a small agricultural, or farming, nation to a powerful, modern nation with many industries and businesses.

The Preamble, which is the short introduction to the Constitution, states:

"We the people of the United States, in order to form a more perfect Union, establish justice, insure domestic tranquility, provide for the common defense, promote the general welfare, and secure the blessings of liberty to ourselves and our posterity, do ordain and establish this Constitution for the United States of America."

The document goes on to explain the goals and purpose of the Constitution. The people of the United States, living under the Constitution, could expect *justice*, peace, and safety at home, and protection from other countries. All these things would be provided by the new Constitution.

The Constitution of the United States

Preamble — Goals and Purpose

Article I — Legislative

Article II — Executive

Article III — Judicial

Article IV — States

Article V — Amendments

Article VI — Supreme Law

Article VII — Ratification

Amendments 1 through 10,
The Bill of Rights (1791)

1. Freedom of religion, speech, press, petition, and assembly

2. Right to bear arms; states to have militia

3. Freedom from having to quarter soldiers in time of peace

4. No unreasonable searches and seizures

5. Grand jury, double jeopardy, and due process

6. Fair trial in criminal cases

7. Jury trial in most civil cases

8. Reasonable bail, fines, and punishment

9. Protection of rights not written in Constitution

10. Power to states or people if not given to federal government

Amendments 11 through 26

11. Protection of states from federal lawsuits (1795)
12. Separate ballots for president and vice president (1804)
13. End of slavery in all states (1865)
14. Citizenship for blacks (1868)
15. Voting rights for blacks (1870)
16. Income tax (1913)
17. Direct election of senators in their own states (1913)
18. Prohibition of liquor (1919)
19. Voting rights for women (1920)
20. Dates for Congress to begin and for president to take office (1933)
21. The end of Prohibition (1933)
22. Limits a president to two elected terms (1951)
23. Voting rights for citizens of Washington, D.C. in presidential elections (1961)
24. End of poll tax (1964)
25. Filling the offices of president and vice president if they become vacant (1967)
26. Eighteen-year-olds may vote in all elections (1971)

The first three articles show how the principle of separation of powers would be followed. Three branches of the federal government would be set up with certain powers and duties

Article I (One): The Legislative Branch

Section 1. *All legislative powers herein granted shall be vested in a Congress of the United States, which shall consist of a Senate and House of Representatives.*

This means Congress has the power to make laws. It further says that the Congress has two parts — a Senate and a House of Representatives.

Executive Powers

The executive branch's job is to carry out the law. Through the Constitution, the president:

- Is commander in chief of the armed forces.
- Has the ability to make treaties, provided two-thirds of the senators agree.
- Shall nominate ambassadors, judges of the Supreme Court, and other public officers.
- Shall give to the Congress information on the state of the union, and recommend measures for them to consider.

Article II (Two): The Executive Branch

Section 1. *(1) The executive power shall be vested in a President of the United States of America. He shall hold his office during the term of four years, and together with the Vice President, chosen for the same term, be elected...*

The many duties of the office are explained in this article, including the power to appoint ambassadors to foreign countries, and judges to the Supreme Court.

Article III (Three): The Judicial Branch

Section 1. *The judicial power of the United States, shall be vested in one Supreme Court, and in such inferior courts as the Congress may from time to time ordain and establish...*

The types of cases which come under the federal courts are outlined in Article III.

ARTICLE IV (Four): How the States Should Treat Each Other

The laws and other legal rulings of one state must be recognized by all other states. This principle is clearly explained in Article IV of the Constitution. Article IV also says that the rights a citizen has in one state will be respected in all states. Finally in this article concerning the states, the federal government guarantees each state a form of government which includes three separate branches of organization, just as the federal system has: legislative (state legislature), executive (governor), and judicial (courts).

★Activity A: Number your paper from 1 to 7. Read each statement. Decide which article of the Constitution made this provision. Write the article number (one of the first four articles) beside the number.

1. A Congress is established or set up.
2. A citizen's rights are respected in all states.
3. Congress shall consist of a Senate and House of Representatives.
4. Each state has three separate branches of government.
5. A president will hold his term of office for four years.
6. The highest judicial power of the United States shall be vested in (given to) the Supreme Court.
7. The president has the power to appoint ambassadors to foreign countries.

PART 2 ★ ★ ★ Articles Five Through Seven

W O R D S   T O   K N O W
Convention   *Majority*

Any change to the Constitution is called an amendment. The writers of the Constitution knew that changes might have to be made from time to time in this important document. Often words had to be added or taken out of the Constitution. Article V (Five) was added so that changes could be made when necessary.

Amendments are proposed in order to make corrections or to add something new. These changes are not easily made. By one method, an amendment is suggested in Congress. This suggestion must then be approved by a two-thirds (2/3) *majority* vote in both the Senate and House of Representatives. This suggestion for a change is then sent to all the states. Three-fourths (3/4) of the state legislatures (lawmaking bodies) must ratify, or approve, the change. If this happens, the change is added to the Constitution as an official amendment.

By using another method for making an amendment, Congress can order special meetings of state *conventions*. Three-fourths of these conventions must vote "yes" to approve a new amendment.

Through the years, more than 9,000 amendments have been suggested, but only twenty-six have been added to the Constitution since it was written in 1787. All but one of the amendments have been approved by state legislatures. The one exception was the 21st Amendment which ended Prohibition, the law that banned the manufacture, use, or transportation of alcoholic beverages. This amendment was approved by constitutional conventions in three-fourths of the states.

ARTICLES VI (Six) and VII (Seven)

Article VI (Six) of the Constitution declares that the Constitution is the supreme, or highest, law of the land. All officials of both the federal and state governments are sworn under oath to support and obey the Constitution.

Article VII (Seven) tells how the ratification of the document will take place. It says that the thirteen states should hold conventions. At least nine of the states must approve the Constitution before it may be used.

★**Activity B:** Number your paper from 1 to 7. Read each statement. Select an answer from the list below that completes the sentence. Write your answer beside each number.

seven   *state convention*
Congress   *something new*
1787   *Six*
nine of the thirteen

1. The Constitution contains ___ articles.
2. Amendments can make corrections or add ___.
3. The Constitution was written in the year ___.
4. An amendment can be suggested in ___ or a ___.
5. Article ___ made the Constitution the supreme law of the land.
6. In order for the Constitution to be ratified, ___ states had to vote for it.

PART 3 ★ ★ ★ The Bill of Rights

The Constitution was not approved at first because it did not guarantee the rights of individuals. A promise was made at the Constitutional Convention to add a part that would guarantee people the rights they wanted, including the right to worship as they pleased and the right of free speech. This promise caused many people to vote in favor of the Constitution.

James Madison, then a member of the House of Representatives, made the first move to see that a list of rights was added to the Constitution. He suggested nine amendments that would strengthen the Constitution. Other suggestions were also made, and finally Congress wrote twelve amendments. These were sent to the states for approval. It took two years for the states to ratify the new amendments, and then only ten of the twelve were approved. These first ten amendments, known as the Bill of Rights, were added to the end of the Constitution. They guaranteed to the people most basic freedoms, including freedom of religion, freedom of speech, and trial by jury.

The First Amendment

The purpose of the First Amendment is to allow people to *express* themselves. This right of free expression is considered by many to be the most important freedom guaranteed by the Constitution.

"Congress shall make no law respecting an establishment of religion, or prohibiting the free exercise thereof; or abridging the freedom of speech, or of the press; or the right of the people peaceably to assemble, and to petition the Government for a redress of grievances."

First of all, the First Amendment guarantees people the right to worship as they please, or not to worship at all. Also, the government may not give public tax money or other support to any one religion.

Second, the First Amendment guarantees to all people the right to express themselves either by the spoken or written word. When some people express themselves, their words offend others; but in a free country, this is allowed. The writers of the amendments felt that by

THE FIRST AMENDMENT AND SUPREME COURT DECISIONS

HIGHLIGHT
STORY

★ ★ ★

Questions come up from time about the First Amendment and its guarantees of individual rights. The Supreme Court has the job of deciding what the First Amendment means in certain cases. Freedom of religion was questioned in the issues of school prayer and financial aid to parochial (religious) schools. When the issues were brought to the Supreme Court, it ruled that it is unconstitutional (illegal) to have students recite a prayer, even if it was written by school officials and did not favor any one religion. The Court said this went against the separation of government and religion as stated in the First Amendment. On the issue of financial aid, the Court ruled that money may be given to parochial schools only for non-religious things, such as lunches, bus rides, textbooks, and counseling.

Freedom of speech has been limited during wartime. During World War I, Congress passed a law forbidding disloyal speech about the government, Constitution, army, navy, the flag, or uniforms. The Supreme Court ruled that this law was legal and constitutional.

Students who write for high school newspapers have been denied freedom of the press. School officials would not allow certain things to be printed if the ideas criticized the school. The Supreme Court said, "Students do not shed their constitutional rights of free expression at the schoolhouse gate." This means that students do have the freedom to express their ideas.

Review
Write the answers to the following questions in complete sentences.
1. When there is a question concerning the rights of an individual as written in the First Amendment, who decides if the action is constitutional or not?
2. What did the Supreme Court decide concerning the reciting of prayers in school?
3. When can parochial schools receive financial aid from the government, according to the ruling of the Supreme Court?
4. When did Congress pass a law limiting the freedom of speech?
5. What did the Supreme Court decide about high school students who criticize their schools in the school newspaper?

allowing the freedom of speech, many different *opinions* would be heard. The best opinions could be accepted by the people.

The United States has a few ways that stops people from speaking freely. Laws exist against slander (spoken false statements) and libel (written false statements), which may hurt someone's reputation. Speeches to promote violence or to endanger public safety are also restricted.

Freedom of the press is the third guarantee in the First Amendment. This means that not only can people speak freely, they can write down their opinions. These opinions can then be circulated in newspapers, magazines, pamphlets, and on radio and television. People also have the right to be informed. In the United States, the press is not owned by the government, but is owned by private individuals or groups of persons. The press can print what it believes to be true and fair.

The fourth guarantee in the First Amendment is the right to *assemble* in groups in a peaceful way and for peaceful purposes. In some countries this is not allowed. Any group in the United States has the right to hold meetings, whether its ideas are popular or not. Outdoor or indoor meetings and demonstrations are permitted. If these events take away the rights of any other citizen, then they are stopped.

The fifth and last guarantee in the First Amendment is the right to *petition*. This means that government officials may be asked to do something or to stop doing something. These petitions, or requests, may come from individuals or from groups. They may be letters or formal written requests. Group petitions may also be prepared and signed by many people and sent to government officials. The petitions may ask a senator, for example, to work to get a certain law passed. People often send petitions to ask that something be stopped, such as the building of a highway or a shopping center.

★**Activity C:** Number your paper from 1 to 6. Choose the correct word from the two given in each sentence. Write the correct word by the number.

1. The government (may, may not) favor one religion over another.
2. We have laws in this country (for, against) slander and libel.
3. The press (is, is not) owned by the government in the United States.
4. Special interest groups in the United States (can, cannot) hold meetings if their ideas are unpopular.
5. Group petitions (may, may not) be sent to government officials.
6. Many people consider the First Amendment to be the (most, least) important amendment to the Constitution.

PART 4 ★ ★ ★ **Second Through Tenth Amendments**

W O R D S	T O	K N O W
Civil		Indict
Evidence		Warrant
Grand jury		Witness

The next two amendments to the Constitution were added to protect Americans from things that had happened in the past. During the Revolutionary War, the British tried to take weapons away from the colonists. This made the colonists feel helpless because they needed the guns to serve in their state militias. A militia is an organized group of citizens who serve as soldiers during a war. The Second Amendment not only gives the people the right to bear arms (weapons), but also the right to use them when serving in the militia. This amendment also permits a state to train and keep a militia for protection in time of need.

The British forced the colonists to quarter (house) soldiers in their homes. Many colonists did this against their will. The Third Amendment protects people from this. It states:

"No soldier shall, in time of peace, be quartered in any house,..."

The Fourth Amendment: Searches and Seizures

In the early days of the United States, the people in authority felt free to enter and search private homes. Sometimes the searchers were looking for stolen or smuggled goods. Many times they were acting on "hunches," and innocent people were made to look guilty. People wanted to feel safe and secure in their homes. The Fourth Amendment does not completely stop searches and seizures, but it does set definite rules about how they are to be done.

Wiretapping and "Bugging"

When the words "unreasonable searches and seizures" were written in the Fourth Amendment, there were no telephones. Later, private telephone conversations could be tapped (secretly listened to) when evidence was needed for a criminal case. Some people felt that this tapping was illegal because it was an "unreasonable search." The Supreme Court ruled in 1928 that phone-tapping was legal, but all the justices did not agree. Some said people had the "right to be let alone...no intrusion by the government on privacy..." It took many years but finally in 1967, the Court ruled that the Fourth Amendment protects people, not just buildings, against "unreasonable searches and seizures." No wiretapping or electronic "bugs" are now permitted unless the court orders it in advance.

The amendment makes it illegal, except in certain cases, to search someone's house without a *warrant*. This warrant must describe the place to be searched and what things might be seized.

The Fifth Amendment states, in part:

"No person shall be held to answer for a capital, or otherwise infamous crime, unless on a presentment or indictment of a grand jury,..."

When a person is accused of a capital (serious) crime, he is first brought before a *grand jury*. This jury listens to the charges and studies the *evidence* given. If the citizens serving on the grand jury decide there is enough evidence, the person is indicted and stands trial for the crime. A person cannot stand trial until the grand jury *indicts* him.

"...nor shall any person be subject for the same offense to be twice put in jeopardy..."

When a person goes on trial for a crime, it is said that his life or freedom is in jeopardy, or danger. According to this amendment, a person does not have to go through this danger a second time because he may not be tried twice for the same crime. It protects citizens from double jeopardy. This amendment also guarantees "due process of law." This means that a person must be given a fair trial according to all the rules and procedures set down in the Constitution. The last part of the Fifth Amendment states that the government may not seize a person's land, money, or other property for public use.

The Sixth Amendment protects a person's right to defend himself in a federal court trial. The accused person has the right to:

1. A speedy public trial before a fair jury in the state where the crime took place.
2. Be told of the crime of which he is accused.
3. Have a lawyer to argue the case.
4. Question all *witnesses*.
5. Have witnesses appear, by legal force if necessary, to tell the accused's side of the case.

The Seventh Amendment applies to *civil* lawsuits. A civil case does not involve a crime. It is usually a dispute between two or more parties over rights or duties. According to this amendment, if the value being disputed is more than twenty dollars, the civil lawsuit is brought to trial before a jury.

The Eighth Amendment was added to limit the amount of bail set by a judge, or fines a person must pay for breaking certain laws. Bail is a sum of money that an accused person must deposit for the privilege of staying out of jail while waiting for the case to come to trial. The judge decides on the amount of bail, usually according to the seriousness of the crime and the reputation of the accused. The reason for bail is to be sure that the person will appear for his trial. This money is returned to the person when the trial begins.

This amendment also states, "...nor cruel and unusual punishments inflicted." This means that punishments such as torture are not allowed. A military court stopped an old Navy punishment of three days on bread and water because the punishment was "cruel and unusual."

Amendments Nine and Ten

Amendments Nine and Ten were added so that all rights not listed directly in the Constitution would belong to the people or to the states. The following words of the Tenth Amendment assure people of these rights and make the people and the states partners in our federal system of government.

"The powers not delegated to the United States by the Constitution, nor prohibited by it to the states, are reserved to the states respectively, or to the people."

Americans also have other freedoms: the right to live and travel anywhere, the right to hold a job, the right to receive an education and marry, and the right to join a political party or other group.

★**Activity D:** Number your paper from 1 to 10. Match the beginning of the sentence in Part 1 with the correct ending in Part 2. Write the complete sentence on your own paper.

Part 1, Beginning of Sentences

1. A person accused of a serious, or capital, crime...
2. "Due process of law" means...
3. The Fourth Amendment says that in order to search someone's home...
4. A militia is an...
5. The Third Amendment protects people from...
6. According to the Fifth Amendment, a person tried for a crime may not...
7. Under the Fifth Amendment the government may not seize...
8. The Sixth Amendment says an accused person may defend himself...
9. A civil case does not involve a crime but is usually...
10. The ninth and tenth amendments were added to give...

Part 2, Ending of Sentences

a. the authorities will need a search warrant.
b. is first brought before a grand jury.
c. housing soldiers in their homes during peacetime.
d. organized group of citizens who serve as soldiers.
e. be tried for the same crime again (double jeopardy).
f. an accused person must be given a fair trial.
g. private property for public use without paying for it.
h. a dispute between two or more parties.
i. in a court of law and have a lawyer.
j. rights to the people and states.

PART 5 ★ ★ ★ Amendments Eleven Through Fifteen

W O R D S   T O   K N O W
Candidate   *Sued*
Debate

U p until 1860 only two amendments were added to the Constitution. The Eleventh Amendment denied the federal courts, including the Supreme Court, the right to make rulings in state affairs. The matter arose when the state of Georgia was *sued* by two citizens of South Carolina. The federal government stepped in to force Georgia to pay. Georgia refused to pay.

The state said that the federal government was taking away some of its power by ruling in the case. As a result of this case, and to ensure that it would not happen again, the Eleventh Amendment was added to the Constitution.

The Twelfth Amendment changed the system for electing a president and vice president. According to this amendment, separate candidates for each office had to be chosen. In the past all candidates for both offices were on the same list. The *candidate* getting the highest number of votes was elected president. The second-place candidate was elected vice president. Problems arose with this system, and one election resulted in a tie. The addition of the Twelfth Amendment, calling for separate candidates for each office, solved this problem. The House of Representatives chooses a winner if neither candidate receives a majority of votes.

Slavery in the United States

Both in 1863, and at the end of the war between the North and South (the Civil War), President Lincoln declared that the slaves in the Confederate States (Southern states) were free men. Congress wrote the Thirteenth Amendment to end slavery. The issue of slavery had been one of the causes of trouble between the North and South. Congress felt it needed to end the dispute once and for all. By the end of 1865, the amendment was ratified and added to the Constitution.

Slaves were now free, but there was still a *debate* over whether the slaves and other black people could be citizens. The passage of the Fourteenth Amendment settled this debate. The amendment says that all people born in the United States and under its rule are citizens. Foreign-born persons who live in the United States can also become citizens by following certain steps. The Fourteenth Amendment also says that the states must follow "due process" and give all citizens "equal protection," just as the federal government does.

The Fifteenth Amendment was the last of the amendments that was passed soon after the Civil War ended. It gave all male Americans the right to vote. The Northern states approved the amendment right away, but the Southern states, except for Tennessee, would not obey the amendment. Congress, using military force, made the Southern states hold conventions. They had to rewrite their state constitutions so that blacks were guaranteed the right to vote.

★**Activity E:** Number your paper from 1 to 10. Complete the following paragraph with words from the box. Write the correct word by the number on your paper.

Civil War	*president*
vote	*vice president*
citizens	*Constitution*
courts	*ended*
slavery	*affairs*

Until 1860 only slight changes were made in the 1)___. Amendment Eleven said the federal 2)___ could not make rulings in state 3)___. Amendment Twelve changed the system for electing a 4)___ and 5)___. After the 6)___, three amendments were added, having to do with 7)___. The Thirteenth Amendment 8)___ slavery in all states. The Fourteenth Amendment said all slaves and black persons could be 9)___. The Fifteenth Amendment gave the right to 10)___ to all males, even former slaves.

PART 6 ★ ★ ★ Amendments Sixteen Through Twenty-six

Forty-three years passed before any more additions were made to the Constitution. From 1913 to 1971, eleven amendments were added. Several amendments have been proposed since 1971, but have failed to pass. Each amendment is listed with a brief statement explaining why it was added.

Sixteen (1913) — To allow Congress the power to pass income tax laws and to collect taxes.

Seventeen (1913) — To allow direct election of senators by the people of their states.

Eighteen (1919) — To end (ban) the making and selling of alcoholic beverages. This was called Prohibition.

Nineteen (1920) — To give women the right to vote.

Twenty (1933) — To set new dates for Congress to begin; to set January 20 as the day the president takes office.

Twenty-one (1933) — To end Prohibition; to give states the decision on whether to ban liquor.

Twenty-two (1951) — To limit the term of president to two elected terms.

Twenty-three (1961) — To allow the citizens of Washington, D.C. to vote for national officials.

Twenty-four (1964) — To end the poll tax (tax paid to vote) in federal elections.

Twenty-five (1967) — To decide who will fill the positions of president and vice president if these persons leave office or become disabled.

Twenty-six (1971) — To set the voting age at 18 in all states.

★**Activity F:** Number your paper from 1 to 10. Select the correct word to complete the sentences.

Twenty-six	*20*
vote	*Twenty-third*
Twenty-one	*poll*
Sixteenth	*18*
two	*alcoholic*

1. Amendment Twenty-six set voting age in all states at ___.
2. A president may be elected to that office no more than ___ times.
3. The Nineteenth Amendment gave women the right to ___.

4. The ___ Amendment allowed the citizens of the nation's capital to vote in national elections.

5. Prohibition banned the making and selling of ___ beverages.

6. Amendment Twenty-four put an end to the ___ tax in federal elections.

7. Amendment ___ put an end to Prohibition.

8. Because of the ___ Amendment, Congress now has the power to pass income tax laws.

9. January ___ is the day the president takes office.

10. So far we have ___ amendments added to the Constitution.

C H A P T E R ★ S U M M A R Y

When the Constitution was ratified by nine of the states, it became the plan of government for the new country. The Preamble states the purpose and goals of the Constitution. The first three articles tell how the federal, or national, government is set up with legislative, executive, and judicial branches. Article Four explains how the states should treat each other. Article Five says that changes can be made in the document when necessary. Article Six declares the Constitution the supreme (highest) law of the land. Article Seven says the Constitution had to be ratified by nine of the thirteen states before it could be put into effect.

The Bill of Rights

Two years after the Constitution was ratified, the first ten amendments were added. These were guarantees of individual rights that were promised at the Constitutional Convention. These first ten amendments are known as the Bill of Rights. Many people consider the First Amendment the most important. It allows people freedom of religion, freedom to express themselves in spoken or written word, and the freedom to assemble peacefully in groups. It also allows people to petition the government for any reason.

Because each state wanted and needed a trained militia made up of citizens who could bear arms, the Second and Third Amendments were added.

The Fourth Amendment protects people in their homes. The next four amendments have to do with the treatment of people accused of crimes. An accused person has to be indicted, then be given a speedy and fair trial, with a lawyer to defend him. Cruel punishment and high fines or bail are not allowed. The last two amendments of the Bill of Rights give to the states and the people any power not given to the national government.

Other Amendments

After the Bill of Rights was added, several years passed with only slight changes in the Constitution. When the Civil War ended in 1865, three important amendments dealing with slavery were approved. The slaves were freed by the Thirteenth Amendment, given their citizenship by the Fourteenth, and then given the right to vote by the Fifteenth.

Another 43 years passed and in the years between 1913 and 1971, Amendments Sixteen through Twenty-six were added to the Constitution. Some of the important changes brought about by these amendments are:

1. Women were allowed to vote.
2. Alcohol was banned, and then later the ban was removed.
3. A president's term of office was limited to two elected terms.
4. The poll, or voting, tax was removed.
5. The voting age was reduced to 18 in all elections.

C H A P T E R ★ R E V I E W

Comprehension:
Identification
Directions: Number your paper from 1 to 10. Choose a word from the list below to complete each sentence. Write the correct word next to each number.

Rights	*Preamble*
women	*articles*
freedoms	*freed*
president	*amendments*
ratified	*accused*

1. The purpose and goals of the Constitution are stated in the ___.
2. The first three ___ tell how the federal government is set up.
3. Article V (Five) said that changes, or ___, could be made when necessary.
4. The Constitution was ___ by nine of the thirteen states.
5. The first ten amendments are known as the Bill of ___.
6. The First Amendment of the Bill of Rights gave people many ___.
7. There are four amendments that have to do with how people ___ of crimes should be treated.
8. The Thirteenth Amendment ___ the slaves.
9. One important amendment gave ___ the right to vote.
10. An amendment was added that said the ___ may be elected to office for only two terms.

Comprehension:
Understanding Main Ideas
Directions: Write the answers to the following questions using complete sentences.

1. According to the Preamble of the Constitution, what could people expect from their newly formed government?
2. What principle of government do the first three articles of the Constitution clearly show?
3. According to Article II of the Constitution, whom may the President appoint and nominate?
4. According to Article IV of the Constitution, how must laws and legal rulings of one state be treated by other states?
5. When and why was the Bill of Rights added to the Constitution?

Critical Thinking:
Write Your Opinion

1. Why do you think Article V is so important to the Constitution?
2. Which of the amendments to the Constitution do you think is the most important to your life?

CHAPTER FOUR

The Legislative Branch

PART 1 The
★ ★ ★ Congress

W O R D S   T O   K N O W

Bill | Representative
Citizen | Serve
Legal | Term
Majority

The federal government of the United States is divided into three separate branches. Each part has special powers granted by the Constitution. One branch is the executive branch. This branch includes the president, vice president, and the president's assistants, or his Cabinet. Another branch is the judicial branch, which is made up of the courts and the judges. The third branch is the legislative branch, which is Congress.

Most of the people who run the federal government meet and work in the capital city, Washington, D.C.

The letters "D.C." stand for the words District of Columbia. Washington, D.C. is located between the states of Maryland and Virginia. The work of the legislative branch is carried on, for the most part, in the United States Capitol Building.

How Congress is Organized

The Congress of the United States is divided into two parts: the House of Representatives and the Senate. The writers of the Constitution did not want one group of officials to become too strong, so they made two parts to the Congress. The men and women who work in these two houses of the Congress are elected by the voters in each state. Every new *bill* for our country must be passed by a *majority* of votes in both the Senate and the House of Representatives. In this way, both houses can carefully study each bill and make better decisions.

The Senate

The writers of the Constitution wanted to be sure that every state would be represented equally in the Congress. Each of the fifty states elects two senators to *serve* in the Senate. Each state, no matter how large or how small its population, has the same number of votes in the Senate as any other state. There are one hundred senators serving in the Senate.

A senator serves a six-year term. Only one-third of the Senate membership are elected at any one time. To run for the Senate, a candidate must be at least thirty years old. He or she must have been a United States citizen for at least nine years. He or she must be a resident of the state he or she represents.

The vice president of the United States serves as the president of the Senate. The vice president does not take part in the debates. He votes only in case of a tie.

The House of Representatives

The House of Representatives is set up to reflect the size of each state's population. States that have more people living in them send more *representatives* to Congress than states that have fewer people. Each state is divided into districts that have about the same number of people, as nearly as is possible. Each district elects its own representative. In this way all citizens are equally represented, despite their state's population. Four hundred and thirty-five elected officials serve in the House of Representatives.

The Legislative branch of government if made up of 100 senators and 435 representatives. Here, President Bush addresses both houses of Congress.

The leader of the House of Representatives is known as the Speaker of the House. The Speaker is one of the representatives who is elected by the majority party members to serve for two years. The Speaker has a strong position, and uses his power to run the House's business.

A member of the House of Representatives serves only a two-year *term*. All of the members of the House are elected in a national election held in November of each even-numbered year. A representative must be at least twenty-five years old. He or she must have been a *citizen* of the United States for at least seven years. The representative must also be a *legal* resident of the state he or she represents. He or she is also expected to live in the district he or she represents.

★**Activity A:** Complete sentences 1 to 3 by writing the missing words on your own paper.

1. The three branches of the federal government are the ____, ____, and the ____.
2. Each of the fifty states has ___ Senators who serve a ___ year term.
3. The total number of representatives who serve in the House of Representatives is ___. Each serves a ___ year term.

In the next section, identify the following Congressmen by writing *S* for Senator or *R* for Representative.

a. Mr. Jacks is 28 and serves the district where he lives.
b. Mr. Todd has been in Congress four years and has been reelected once.
c. Mrs. Ellis is 50 and serves in the smaller house of Congress.
d. Mr. Smith serves the state of California along with 40 other Congressmen.
e. Mr. Lee has been a Congressmen for six years and will run for re-election for the first time.

PART 2 ★ ★ ★ How Congress Does Its Work

W O R D S   T O   K N O W

Adjourn	*Permanent*
Consider	*Political*
Encourage	*Reject*
Foreign	*Session*

The Senate and House of Representatives both begin their sessions in Washington, D.C. early in January of each year. The sessions last until the work is completed. Each year Congress takes longer and longer to finish its job. Sometimes Congress does not *adjourn* until late fall. Near the end of the sessions, the senators and representatives vote on a day to adjourn. If a serious problem comes up after Congress has adjourned, the president may ask Congress to come back and hold a special *session*. Such a special session would last until the problem is solved.

Congress' Duties

The most important duty of Congress is to make laws. It has other powers or duties given to it by the Constitution. Congress may suggest amendments to the Constitution. The process, however, is not an easy one. The final decision rests with the consent of the states. Congress can investigate or check on the other two branches of the federal government. This inves-tigation may take place if one of the departments of the government is thought to be doing something wrong. Taxes, the armed forces, trade, and certain crimes are some of the other things taken care of by Congress.

Floor Leaders

In order for the Senate and House to do their work well, they must have good leaders. "Floor" leaders are chosen during the early part of the sessions. These floor leaders are very important because they tell other senators and representatives about the new bills that will be voted on. They also *encourage* the other members to take part in the voting. They work closely with the Speaker of the House and the president of the Senate to manage debates and committee business.

Bills Are Plans for New Laws

During every session of Congress, the members study a great number of bills. A bill is an idea for a new law or a change in an old law. The idea can come from a citizen who writes a senator or a representative with the suggestion. An idea can come from special groups, such as businessmen, veterans, or parents' groups. The president of the United States can also suggest ideas for bills. Senators and representatives can suggest ideas for new laws, as well.

Bills Are Numbered

A new bill can be introduced in either the Senate or the House. It is carefully typed, and each line is numbered. In this way every part of the bill is easy to find if it needs to be changed. The whole bill is also given a number and letters. For example,

H.R. 505 means that the bill was introduced in the House of Representatives and that is the five hundred and fifth bill to be studied during that session.

Work Is Done in Committee

Thousands of bills are considered by Congress each year. It would not be possible for all of the members to look at all these bills. Therefore the work of studying the bills is turned over to many smaller groups, or committees. Committees decide which bills are important enough to send to the House or Senate for all members to *consider*. Many bills are *rejected* by committees and never given further consideration.

Each part of Congress has a number of *permanent* commit-tees called standing committees. Each considers a specific topic, such as how we get along with *foreign* governments. Another commit-tee takes care of the needs of the armed services. Another decides how to raise money for running the fed-eral government. This committee is called the Ways and Means Committee.

There are also special committees which are formed just for certain purposes and then dismissed. A few committees are made up of members

Filibusters in the Senate

Before a bill can become a law it must be approved by a majority of the members of both houses of Congress. As you can imagine, not all Congressmen agree on all parts of every bill. Most of the time, the Senators and Representatives take part in long and heated debates concerning the bills. These debates are important in order to hear all sides of an issue. Once the bill is approved by Congress and the President, it will become a new law. This work of Congress concerning bills and laws is very important.

In the Senate, but not in the House, a bill may be debated as long as necessary. A Senator who is strongly opposed to a bill and wants to delay a vote, may talk on and on. There is no limit to the amount of time he talks. This long and rambling style of talking is called "filibustering." In the history of the Senate, there have been some very long filibusters, some lasting almost 25 hours.

from both the Senate and the House of Representatives. These are called joint committees.

All Members of Congress Serve on Committees

Each senator and representative must serve on at least one standing committee. He or she is asked to serve on a committee by special groups from *political* parties. Members of Congress always hope to be put on important committees, such as the Foreign Affairs, Ways and Means, and Armed Services committees. Some members serve on two or three committees. The longer a member serves on a committee, the more likely he or she is to become its leader, or chairperson. This practice is called the "seniority system." Even though changes in this system were made in the 1970s, seniority is still very important.

★**Activity B:** Number your paper from 1 to 6. Choose the correct ending for each sentence from the two endings given. Write the letter you choose next to each number.

1. The idea for a bill
   (a) can come from a citizen, groups, or members of Congress.
   (b) cannot come from members of Congress.

2. Each member of Congress
   (a) decides whether or not to serve on a committee.
   (b) must serve on at least one standing committee.

3. Congress has permanent committees that
   (a) can never change anything in a bill.
   (b) consider specific topics such as the armed services.

4. Committees decide if the bills are important enough to send to
   (a) the president.
   (b) other members of the Senate or House.

5. Joint committees
   (a) are made up of members from the Senate and the House.
   (b) make bills into law.

HOW A BILL BECOMES A LAW

Anyone may suggest the idea for a new law to a member of Congress. Members of Congress may give ideas for new bills. The president often expresses to Congress his feelings about the need for new laws in his State of the Union Message. This speech is given by the president at the start of each new session of Congress in January.

A bill may begin either in the House or in the Senate. If an idea for a new bill begins in the House of Representatives, a representative writes out a proposed bill and gives it to the Clerk of the House. The Clerk assigns it a number and reads the title to the members. The title is printed in the *Congressional Record* (a quarterly publication that lists all business carried on by Congress). This action is called the first reading. The Clerk sends the bill to be printed so that all members and interested persons may have copies. The bill is then sent by the Speaker of the House to the proper standing committee for study. The committee may change it if necessary, or put it aside for while (pigeonhole it). If the committee likes the bill, it will approve it and send it back to the House with a good report. The bill is given a date when it will be voted on. If a majority of representatives vote in favor of it, the bill is then sent to the Senate and given a number. The same procedures are followed as in the first house.

A new bill follows the same steps to become a law, whether it starts in the House or in the Senate. There is a difference, however, in the amount of time allowed for

★　★　★

debate. House debate is limited, but senators may debate as long as they wish. A senator can delay voting on a bill by talking on and on, sometimes for many hours. This way of putting off a vote is called filibustering.

After the bill is passed by the House and Senate, it is sent to the president. When a bill reaches the president's desk, he has several choices:

1. He can accept and sign the bill.
2. He can do nothing and let the bill become a law without signing it. The bill automatically becomes a law after ten working days while Congress is in session.
3. He can *veto* the bill and refuse to sign it. If the president vetoes a bill, it can still become a law if it is approved by a two-thirds majority of the members of Congress.
4. He can let a bill die if Congress adjourns before a 10 day period has elapsed. This is called a "pocket veto."

Review

Directions: If a bill begins in the House of Representatives it goes through certain steps before it reaches the president's desk. Write these steps in the correct order on your own paper.

a. A bill is given a date to be voted on.
b. Senate approves the bill.
c. The clerk numbers the bill and sends it to the proper committee.
d. If the representatives vote for the bill, it is sent to the Senate.
e. A committee studies and approves the bill.
f. The bill is sent to the President.

PART 3 ★★★ Powers of Congress

W O R D S   T O   K N O W

Admitted   *Nobility*
Defend   *Power*

Article I, Section 8 of the Constitution lists the powers of Congress. Some of those powers are described here:

1. The federal government needs a great deal of money to carry on its work. Congress can raise and collect taxes to pay for the salaries of government employees and to maintain government functions. The government also has programs that care for the poor, old, sick, and handicapped.

2. Congress watches over trade and business activities and passes laws to protect business and consumers. Congress runs the system of national highways. These roads help businesses in our country move their products across the whole nation.

3. Congress *defends* the nation against enemies. It can declare war. It established the army and navy.

4. Congress may set standards of weights and measures.

5. Congress passes laws to tell people from other countries how they may become citizens. Congress also decides how new states are *admitted* to the United States.

Limits on the Congress

The writers of the Constitution restricted the *power* of Congress. For example, Congress might pass a bill and it is signed into law. Then if the Supreme Court says that the law goes against the Constitution, the law is taken away.

Congress cannot make laws about such things as elections, education, or marriage. The Constitution gave the states the power to control those things. Congress cannot make laws that take away the rights of citizens. These rights were granted by the Bill of Rights. The Bill of Rights is made up of the first ten amendments to the Constitution. The Bill of Rights guarantees to citizens the basic rights, such as freedom of religion, freedom of speech, and freedom of the press.

Congress cannot take money from the federal government without passing a law to do so. It cannot grant titles of *nobility* (king, queen, or prince) because the American people believe that "all men are created equal."

The "Elastic Clause" of the Constitution Stretches the Power of Congress

The writers of the Constitution knew that problems would come up that were not mentioned in the Constitution. Therefore the Constitution has an "elastic clause." The last part of Article I, Section 8 tells Congress that it can make all laws necessary for carrying out its duties. In other words, Congress is able to make changes, or be flexible when making decisions. For example, Congress was given the power to set up an army and navy to protect the citizens. After a few years Congress saw that in order to have the best army and navy, military colleges were needed to train officers for services. Congress passed a law that gave money to set up and run military colleges. Two of the best known are the U.S. Military Academy at West Point, New York, and the U.S. Naval Academy at Annapolis, Maryland. These are examples of how Congress used the "elastic clause" of the Constitution to stretch its power.

Congress used the "elastic clause" to establish the United States Naval Academy at Annapolis, Maryland.

★**Activity C:** Number your paper from 1 to 10. Choose the best word to complete each sentence. Write the word next to the number on your paper.

1. Congress can raise and collect (roads, taxes, programs) to pay the employees of the federal government.
2. The government has special (needs, crimes, programs) that care for the sick, poor, and handicapped.
3. Congress may set the standards for weights and (temperatures, measures, heights).
4. Through its power, Congress has set up the army and navy to (collect, defend, declare) our country.
5. Congress set up a system of national highways through the (place, power, nation) given to it by the Constitution.
6. Congress has the power to (weigh, declare, raise) war.
7. People from other countries may want to become (citizens, Congress, nobility) of the United States.
8. (Washington, D.C., Congress, Capital) can decide how new states are admitted to our country.
9. Congress cannot make laws about (marriage, taxes, business).
10. The "elastic clause" allows Congress to make (problems, changes, decisions) in the Constitution.

C H A P T E R ★ S U M M A R Y

In this chapter you learned that the legislative branch is one of the three branches of the federal, or national, government. The other two branches are the executive and the judicial.

The main job of the legislative branch is to propose legislation that affects all of the states, and the country as a whole. Each state in the United States can also make certain laws for itself. The Constitution has given the legislative branch the power to make laws.

The lawmaking body of the legislative branch is called the Congress. Congress is divided into two separate parts: the Senate and the House of Representatives. The people of this country elect the men and women who work in the Senate and the House. The citizens of each state elect their own senators and representatives, who represent them in Congress.

Every January all of the senators and representatives go to Washington, D.C. to begin their work. Leaders are chosen for each part of Congress. In order to carry out their tasks, the senators and representatives work in committees. The committees study all of the new bills that are given to them. Usually changes are made in the bills before they are voted on. After one part of the Congress passes a bill, it must be passed by the other part of Congress. Then the president must consider it. If the president signs the bill, it becomes a law for our country.

Congress is an important group of people. The Constitution granted Congress special powers. Some of these powers include collecting taxes, taking care of trade, and providing for defense.

The writers of the Constitution did not want Congress to become too powerful. Therefore they limited the powers of Congress. Congress cannot do the following: pass laws that take away individual rights given by the Bill of Rights, interfere with state laws, or take money from the government without passing a law.

To make sure that Congress had the power to do everything needed to carry out its duties, an "elastic clause" was included in the Constitution. This gives Congress the power to take action as times change, even if this power is not written in the Constitution. However this action cannot take away states' rights or a person's rights.

C H A P T E R ★ R E V I E W

Comprehension:
Identification

Directions: Use the following words to complete the paragraph below about the legislative branch. Number your paper from 1 to 10. Write the correct word next to each number.

vote   elected
considered   reject
veto   introduced
population   majority
committee   session

The number of representatives from each state is determined by the size of the state's 1)___. There are two senators from each state. Senators and representatives are 2)___ by voters in their own states. These congress-members meet in January each year to begin a 3)___. Each senator and representative must serve on at least one 4)___ during a session. Thousands of new bills are 5)___ in Congress each year. After a bill is 6)___ by a committee, two things may happen to it. The committee can 7)___ the bill. They will do this if they find the bill of little use. The committee can accept the bill and give it to the whole Senate or House to consider and 8)___ on. If a 9)___ of the members vote in favor of the bill, the bill is sent to the other house of Congress to be considered. The bill must be passed by both houses of Congress before it can go to the president. The president may accept or 10)___ the bill.

Comprehension:
Understanding Main Ideas

Directions: Write the answers to the following questions using complete sentences.

1. How many parts is the Congress divided into and what is each part called?
2. How is it decided how many members each part of Congress will have?
3. What is the difference in the length of term between a Senator and a Representative?
4. List the requirements for Senators and Representatives.
5. Where do ideas for bills come from?

Critical Thinking:
Writing Your Opinion

1. Do you think the elastic clause of the Constitution is important? Why or why not?
2. Can you think of any situation which might cause the President to call Congress back for a special session after they have adjourned?

CHAPTER FIVE

The Executive Branch

PART 1 ★ ★ ★ What Is the Executive Branch?

WORDS TO KNOW
Adviser
Agency
Responsible
Staff

The executive branch is one of the three departments of the federal government. The executive branch carries out, or enforces, the laws made by the legislative branch. The president is in charge of the executive branch.

In this chapter you will learn about the office of the presidency and how it works as part of the executive branch.

The President Is the Leader of the Executive Branch

The president of the United States is not only the leader of the nation but also the leader of the executive branch. He is sometimes called the "chief executive." His job is difficult because he (or she) is *responsible* for everything that is done by the different groups who work in this branch of the government.

The president needs many assistants in the executive branch to help him carry out the laws. His main helper is the vice president. The vice president becomes president if for any reason the president cannot carry out his duties. The president also has a *staff* of *advisers* that he depends upon. These advisers do everything from answering the mail to planning the president's busy schedule.

There are many departments and *agencies* within the executive branch. The men and women in these special groups carry out the day-to-day work. The president has to know what goes on in all his departments and agencies. He has the final responsibility for all that happens in the executive branch.

Departments and Agencies of the Executive Branch

Executive Office
Office of Management and Budget
National Security Council
Council on Economic Policy
Council of Economic Advisers
White House Office
Council on Environmental Quality
Office of National Drug Control Policy
National Space Council
Office of Policy Development
(and many others)

Cabinet
Department of State (1789)
Department of the Treasury (1789)
Department of Defense (1789)
Department of Justice (1870)
Department of the Interior (1849)
Department of Agriculture (1862)
Department of Labor (1913)
Department of Commerce (1903)
Department of Housing and Urban Development (1965)
Department of Transportation (1966)
Department of Energy (1977)
Department of Health and Human Services (1979)
Department of Education (1979)
Department of Veterans Affairs

Agencies and Commissions
Federal Reserve System
Federal Communications Commission
Federal Trade Commission
Interstate Commerce Commission
United States Information Agency
Environmental Protection Agency
(and many others)

★Activity A: Number your paper from 1 to 8. Next to each number write the words that complete the sentence. Use words from the list below.

assistant   *executive branch*
agencies   *chief executive*
president   *schedule*
responsible   *vice president*
departments   *advisers*

1. The part of the federal government that carries out the laws of the nation is the ___.
2. The vice president is the president's main ___.
3. The ___ is in charge of all parts of the executive branch.
4. The president is sometimes called the ___.
5. The president's job is difficult because he is ___ for all that happens within the executive branch.
6. The ___ becomes president if for any reason the president cannot carry out his duties.
7. The president has a staff of ___ to help him with his busy ___.
8. There are many ___ and ___ to carry out the work of the executive branch.

The Process to Elect a President

W O R D S   T O   K N O W

Candidate	*Qualification*
Definite	*Representative*
Elector	*Select*

With just a few words, the writers of the Constitution set up the powerful office of president. Article II of the Constitution begins:

Section 1. (1) *The executive power shall be vested in a President of the United States.*

The Constitution goes on to explain in more detail the full power of the president. Throughout the years much has been added to Article II to make the duties of the president more *definite*.

Qualifications of a President

The Constitution says that a *candidate* for president must have certain *qualifications*. They are:

1. He or she must be a native-born American citizen.
2. He or she must be at least 35 years of age.
3. He or she must have been a resident of the United States for at least 14 years.

The President Is Elected Every Four Years

Every four years on the Tuesday following the first Monday in November, the people of the United States vote for president and vice president. This day is called Election Day. After campaigns that last many months, it is time for the people to vote for their choices. Each person is guaranteed the right to vote in secret. This is done in the privacy of a voting booth.

Article II and the Twelfth Amendment describe how the president and vice president are to be elected. Votes for the president and vice president are really votes for *electors*. Each state has the same number of electors as it has senators and *representatives*. They are *selected* by political parties, each of which names candidates. As a group these electors are called the electoral college. A count of votes on or shortly after the election day shows who will be president or vice president. However, the electoral college must meet in December and make the election official by voting for the candidates they have promised to support.

By receiving a majority of the electoral votes, George Bush was elected President of the United States in 1988.

A President May Not Be Elected to More Than Two Terms of Office

The limit of two terms of office was set by the Twenty-second Amendment to the Constitution. Before this was passed, Franklin Roosevelt had been elected four times, starting in 1932. This was the main

TRUMAN'S SURPRISE VICTORY IN 1948 PRESIDENTIAL ELECTION

HIGHLIGHT STORY

★ ★ ★

Vice President Harry S. Truman became President the first time only because President Roosevelt died shortly after being elected to his fourth term. During this time Truman gained a reputation for being a hard worker, having good common sense, and being dedicated to his public office. He also became known for his ability to make bold decisions under pressure. After the war in Europe ended, things changed for Truman and his Democratic Party. Although they had handled most postwar problems well, they were still blamed for the country's depression. According to a Gallop Poll, Truman's popularity had fallen to only 32 percent and now it was time for the presidential election of 1948.

The Republicans were sure they could defeat Truman. Thomas E. Dewey was nominated as the Republican candidate. The Democrats were badly divided and many did not want Truman, but eventually he won the nomination. Truman began his campaign by severely criticizing the Republican Congress, which he referred to as "good for nothings." He announced to his Democratic party that "he would win this election and make the Republicans like it!"

Truman decided to take his personal message directly to the people, especially the farmers and workers of the country. He took off by train on a six-week, "whistle stop" tour of the country. He stopped at hundreds of small towns where large numbers of people came out to hear his candid, down-to-earth speeches. In Ohio alone, crowds of up to 10,000 people jammed the small railway stations. When it was over, the election results shocked and surprised most people, except Truman. Some newspapers had even printed headlines announcing Dewey's victory the night before the election. Truman's defeat of Dewey was one of the biggest political upsets in history — Truman had captured 303 electoral votes, while Dewey had only 189.

Review

Directions: On your own paper, answer these questions using complete sentences.

1. How did Truman become President the first time?
2. What was the condition of the country after the war in Europe?
3. Who was the Republican candidate for President in 1948?
4. Why do you think the Republicans thought they could defeat Truman and the Democrats?
5. What was Truman's plan to win the election of 1948? Was it successful?

reason a limit was put on the number of times a person could run for president. George Washington, our first president, had the chance to run for a third term. He refused because he believed changing the presidency was for the good of the country. He believed new ideas would keep the country strong.

★Activity B: Number your paper from 1 to 8. Write the answer to each question.

1. What article of the Constitution established the office of the president?
2. How old must a candidate for president be?
3. How long must a person be a resident of the United States before running for the office of president?
4. How often do the voters in the United States elect a president and a vice president?
5. How is voting done in the United States?
6. How many electors does each state have?
7. How many terms may a president be elected to office?
8. Which amendment tells the number of terms allowed for a person to be president?

PART 3 ★★★ Duties of the President

W O R D S	T O	K N O W
Accused		Legislator
Ambassador		Military
Budget		Resign
Commander		Scandal
Excise		Vacant

As the leader of the executive branch of the government, the president may send armed forces anywhere in the world. For this reason, he is known as the *commander* in chief of the armed forces. He does not actually lead American forces into battle. However, he stays in close touch with the *military* leaders.

Chief Diplomat

The president is also the chief diplomat. He is responsible for the way the United States treats other nations in the world. He tries to keep the country on friendly terms with other countries. The president appoints *ambassadors* to represent the United States in foreign countries. He also welcomes foreign representatives when they visit the United States. Many presidents have traveled around the world to speak to important leaders. They have done this to develop better understanding with the leaders of foreign countries.

Chief Legislator

The president is the chief *legislator*, even though he is not a member of Congress. All bills passed by the Congress must be sent to the president for him to act on. He can also suggest new laws to Congress. Once each year he makes an important speech to both parts of Congress. This is called the "State of the Union Address." In this talk he tells Congress and the whole nation about the condition of the country. He points out what he believes the country will need in the following year. He tells how the government is planning to make any important changes.

The president must also prepare a *budget* for the nation each year. This budget goes before Congress. The members of Congress study it carefully. If they approve it, the president may use this budget in carrying out his plans for running the government. The United States receives money to operate from many resources, including individual and corporation income taxes, social insurance taxes and contributions, *excise* taxes, estate and gift taxes, customs duties, and deposits of earnings in the Federal Reserve Banks.

Political Leader

When the voters elect a president, they also choose a plan for running the government. This plan is made up by the president's political party. For this reason, the president may be called "the chief of his party." The president is expected to follow plans

Every January the president gives the State of the Union Address to Congress and the American people to tell them how the United States is doing and what plans he has for the year ahead.

of his party. He tries to get Congress to put his party's plans into action. The president can use his power to appoint people to jobs important to running the nation. He usually chooses these people from his own political party.

World Leader

Smaller nations of the world look to the leaders of powerful nations for help and guidance. This makes the President of the United States a world leader. What he does is followed and studied by people of other countries and by their leaders. In his role as a world leader, the president must act in the interest of peace. By keeping the United States at peace with other countries, he sets an example for foreign leaders. For example, former President Jimmy Carter acted as a peacemaker when Israel and Egypt were having trouble in 1978. He brought the leaders of these two nations together to discuss a peace plan.

Power to Grant Pardons

A pardon is a legal order given by the president. If a person is guilty of breaking a federal law, the president can pardon that person. This is done only in special instances. The person will not be punished for the crime if he is pardoned. Persons breaking state laws cannot receive a pardon from the president. A pardon is usually granted after the person has been found guilty in court. But the president may pardon a person before the person is tried in court.

This happened in 1974 when President Gerald Ford granted a full pardon to

Acting as a peacemaker, former President Jimmy Carter used his position as a world leader to bring Menachem Begin of Israel and Anwar Sadat of Egypt together to discuss peace between their two countries.

former President Richard Nixon. Nixon had resigned when he was about to be tried. Gerald Ford, the vice president, then became president. Nixon had been involved in a *scandal* called "Watergate," and had been *accused* of breaking the law. He was never tried because he resigned first. When Ford became president he granted Nixon a full pardon. This meant he could not later be tried for the same crime.

The office of president may become *vacant* for several reasons. This has happened six times since 1900. President William McKinley was shot and killed in 1901. President Woodrow Wilson was disabled by a stroke in 1919. Presidents Warren Harding and Franklin Roosevelt died while in office. John F. Kennedy was assassinated in 1963. In 1974 Richard Nixon resigned. He has been the only president to *resign* his office.

Amendment Twenty-five of the Constitution provides for filling a vacancy in the office of president or vice president.

Section 1. *In case of the removal of the president from office or of his death or resignation, the vice president shall become president.*

Section 2. *Whenever there is a vacancy in the office of vice president, the president shall nominate a vice president who shall take office upon confirmation by a majority of both houses of Congress.*

★Activity C: Number your paper from 1 to 6. Choose the best word for each sentence. Write your answers.

1. As commander in chief, the president stays in close touch with (elected, military, weak) leaders.
2. In the "State of the Union" message, the president tells the whole nation about the (Congress, budget, condition) of the country.
3. The president is the leader of his (political, constitutional, annual) party.
4. The President of the United States is the leader of one of the most (undeveloped, powerful, lawless) nations in the world.
5. The president can (elect, appoint, force) people in his political party to jobs.
6. Because the president is head of a strong country, other countries follow what he does. This makes him a (limited, weak, world) leader.

PART 4 ★ ★ ★ People Who Advise the President

WORDS TO KNOW

Economy
Environment
Labor

Natural resources
Security

The president has a group of advisers called the Cabinet. The Cabinet is made up of the heads of the thirteen executive departments. The Cabinet members are in charge of their special departments, and they also offer advice to the president. They are all called Secretaries except for the head of the Justice Department. He is called the Attorney General.

The president appoints the Secretaries and the Attorney General. Special qualifications are carefully considered for each job. The Secretary of Agriculture, for example, is usually a farmer or has a background in agriculture. The Secretary of the Treasury should have financial experience. The Secretary of Housing and Urban Development almost always has experience in city planning.

The Cabinet meets with the president whenever the president decides it is necessary. The meetings usually take place once a week. Reports are made by the Secretaries about important happenings within their departments. Advice is offered to the president at these meetings. Also present at the meetings are the vice president and the heads of some of the agencies of the Executive Office. The meetings are closed to the press and the public.

The Executive Office

The president is assisted by a large group of individuals and agencies called the Executive Office of the President. These people work in offices in the White House and in nearby buildings.

Members of the President's Cabinet

Secretary of State
Secretary of the Treasury
Attorney General
Secretary of the Interior
Secretary of Agriculture
Secretary of Commerce
Secretary of Defense
Secretary of Energy
Secretary of of Education
Secretary of Transportation
Secretary of Housing and Urban Development
Secretary of Health and Human Services
Secretary of Labor
Secretary of Veteran's Affairs

The White House Office

The people closest to the president are in the White House Office. These special assistants advise the president about such important things as foreign affairs, defense, money matters, and the business of Congress. One assistant, called the press secretary, supplies White House news to the press. Another assistant writes the president's speeches. The president also has a personal doctor.

The National Security Council

The National Security Council keeps the president informed about *security,* or safety, matters in the United States. The very secret Central Intelligence Agency works under this council. Its job is to gather information that has to do with the country's security. Agents of the CIA work in all parts of the world and report their findings to the National Security Council.

The Office of Management and Budget

The Office of Management and Budget (OMB) is in charge of preparing the federal budget. This budget is prepared yearly and lists all the money that is expected and the ways it will be spent by the government. When the budget is ready, the president presents it to the Congress for their consideration. In addition to writing the budget, the OMB studies how the executive branch is run. It makes suggestions to the president for improvements and changes.

A President and Vice President Who Were Never Elected

The Constitution states that the two highest executive positions in the country, the president and vice president, are to be elected positions. The vice president takes over if something happens to the president. If something happens to the vice president, the president then appoints a new vice president. Sometimes events occur so rapidly that the results appear to go against the Constitution. This happened in the early 1970s when the offices of president and vice president became filled by two men, neither of whom had been elected.

Spiro Agnew, the vice president under Richard Nixon, resigned in 1973. President Nixon then appointed Gerald Ford as vice president. As events developed in the "Watergate" scandal, President Nixon then chose to resign rather than be brought to trial. This made Vice President Ford the new president, which left the country without a vice president. Ford appointed Nelson Rockefeller to be vice president. This put the country in the hands of two men who had not been chosen by the people, although the actions were done according to the Constitution. This had never happened before in American history.

Council of Economic Advisers

Several agencies within the Executive Office keep the president informed and advised about important matters. The president needs information about the nation's *economy*. He gets it from the Council of Economic Advisers. This small group reports to the president about money matters and also suggests needed programs. The president uses this information in his work and in his reports to Congress and to the American people about our economy.

Council of Environmental Quality

The condition of the *environment* is of great importance to the president. Clean water, clean air, and careful use of *natural resources* are controlled by the government. This is done, in part, by the Council of Environmental Quality.

Other Groups

Several other councils inform the president about foreign trade and *labor* matters. The president is also told about the latest developments in science.

★**Activity D:** Number your paper from 1 to 8. Choose the best word to complete each sentence. Write your answers.

1. The head of the Department of (Labor, Justice, Interior) is called the Attorney General.
2. The heads of all of the other departments have the title (President, Adviser, Secretary).
3. The heads of the executive departments make up the president's (Cabinet, Council, Agency).
4. The Secretary of (Defense, Education, Agriculture) usually has a background in farming.
5. The Cabinet members give advice to the (environment, president, voters).
6. The National Security Council gathers information about the (pollution, security, press) of the nation.
7. The Council on (Economic Advisers, Environmental Quality) informs the president about air pollution.
8. The budget for the nation is prepared, in part, by the (Office of Management and Budget, White House office).

C H A P T E R ★ S U M M A R Y

The executive branch of government carries out the laws made by the Congress. The president of the United States is in charge of the executive branch. He is responsible for everything that takes place in this part of government.

Every four years the citizens of the United States elect a president. In order for a person to be a candidate for president, he or she must be at least thirty-five years of age, a native-born American citizen, and a resident of the United States for fourteen years. The vice president is next in line if the office of the president becomes vacant.

The presidency is the most powerful office in the land. In his job the president has to fill many roles. As leader of the executive branch, he is also commander in chief of the armed forces. He acts as chief diplomat of the United States by keeping on friendly terms with other nations. As chief legislator, he must respond to all the actions of Congress and make suggestions to the Congress. Because he is elected by the voters of his party, he becomes head of his political party. He tries to put his party's plans into action. He appoints people to fill jobs. Many of the people of the world look to the president for guidance. This makes him a world leader.

The president's Cabinet is a group of close advisers. They are the heads of the fourteen executive departments. They meet regularly with the president to keep him informed about matters within their department. The president appoints the heads of these departments.

Directly under the president is the Executive Office. Working within this group is the press secretary, a speech writer, and other assistants who help the president.

C H A P T E R ★ R E V I E W

Comprehension:
Vocabulary

Directions: Listed below are ten words from the chapter. Use them to complete the paragraphs below about the president. Number your paper from 1 to 10. Write the correct word next to each number.

vice president   Cabinet
advisers   environment
Office   electors
responsible   budget
security   appointed

The president holds the most powerful office in the country. He is 1)___ for everything that happens in the executive branch of government. If the office of president becomes vacant, the 2)___ takes over. The president is elected every four years. He is really elected by 3)___ who are chosen from each state.

The president has many 4)___ who assist him in carrying out his duties. The heads of the executive departments are known as the president's 5)___. The Cabinet members are 6)___ by the president. They meet about once a week to advise and inform the president about matters within their departments. The closest advisers to the president are the members of the Executive 7)___. Some of the matters taken care of by this group have to do with the nation's 8)___. Another agency within this office helps the president prepare a plan for taking in and spending money. This plan is called a 9)___. Another agency informs the president about the conditions of the nation's 10)___, including water, air, and land.

Comprehension:
Understanding Main Ideas

Directions: Write the answers to the following questions using complete sentences.
1. During Presidential elections, how are state electors chosen?
2. As a world leader, what are at least two duties of the President?
3. How does the President report on the condition of the country to the Congress and nation?
4. Who makes up the President's Cabinet and what do they do?
5. Name three agencies of the Executive Office and explain the function of each.

Critical Thinking:
Writing Your Opinion

1. Do you think it is right that the President has the power to grant reprieves and pardons for offenses against the United States? Give reasons for your answer.
2. It has been suggested by some that a President serve one six-year term rather than be allowed to serve two four-year terms. Do you think this would be a good idea? Why or why not?

CHAPTER SIX

★ ★ ★

Departments of the Executive Branch

PART 1
★ ★ ★ **Development of the Departments**

WORDS TO KNOW
Commerce   *Urban*
Interior   *Welfare*

George Washington, the United States' first chief executive, did not have all of the assistants that a president now has. The Constitution said that the president should ask for and have the help he needed. Congress provided three departments to meet Washington's needs: State, War, and Treasury. There was also an attorney general to help with matters concerning the law.

The secretaries of the departments, the attorney general, and the vice president often met together with President Washington. This group was the beginning of what later came to be known as the president's Cabinet.

How the Departments Changed and Increased

Today the president's Cabinet is made up of the heads of the fourteen executive departments. They are appointed by the president, but they must be approved by Congress before they can serve.

Through the years more departments were added as they were needed. Some departments were done away with, or combined with others. Between 1798 and 1965, eight departments were added. They were: Navy, Agriculture, Justice, *Commerce*, Post Office, Labor, *Interior*, and Health, Education, and *Welfare* (HEW). HEW has since been divided into two departments—Education, and Health and Human Services. The Defense Department came into being after World War II when the departments of War and Navy were combined.

Since 1965 four other departments have been formed. They are the Department of Housing and *Urban* Development, the Department of Transportation, the Department of Energy, and the Department of Veterans Affairs. In 1971 the Post Office Department was done away with. It was formed into an independent agency, the U.S. Postal Service.

Duties of the Department

Many people in the executive departments work with the Secretaries as they carry out their duties. Each department is made up of smaller units called bureaus, offices, services, or divisions. These offices are not all in Washington, D.C. They are scattered throughout the country where they are needed to serve the people. The Department of Agriculture, for instance, has offices in every state so that it can help farmers and consumers through its many food services.

★**Activity A:** Answer each of the questions using complete sentences on your own paper.

1. What three departments did George Washington have?
2. Who makes up the President's Cabinet?
3. What departments were combined to make up the Defense Department after World War II?
4. What happened to the Post Office Department in 1971?
5. What are the names of two smaller units that make up each department?

GEORGE WASHINGTON — FIRST PRESIDENT AND FIRST STATESMAN

HIGHLIGHT STORY

★ ★ ★

George Washington, known as the "Father of his Country," deserves the title. He served as a military leader during the Revolutionary War. He led the Constitutional Convention and helped write a democratic plan for government. Finally, he was unanimously elected to be the first president of the new country, the United States of America. Many agree that without Washington, the American Revolution and the birth of a new country would not have been successful.

After the war, when a weary Washington had wanted to retire to his plantation at Mount Vernon, he was called to the Constitutional Convention. Because of his strong sense of duty and intense interest in the new country, he did not refuse. After the convention, he again tried to retire to his home. However, the people unanimously elected him president and he was called to serve his country once again. This was the most difficult task of his career. After the triumphant trip from his home in Virginia, to his inauguration in the temporary capital, New York City, Washington faced the difficult problems of running a new nation. As yet, there were no federal laws, no courts, no law-enforcement officers, and serious financial problems. President Washington had to also work out a foreign policy and rebuild the military.

Washington was a true statesman — he had no desire for personal glory or power. He performed all his duties with the welfare of the country and its people in mind. The people wanted him to remain as president until he died, but for the good of the country, he refused to run for a third term. As Douglas Freeman wrote in his biography of Washington, "even his rivals had to admit his superiority of character."

Review

Answer the following questions in complete sentences.

1. What three important roles did Washington play in the history of our country?
2. What title has been given Washington?
3. What were some problems Washington had to face as the first President?
4. Why was Washington considered to be a true statesman?
5. Why did Washington refuse to run for a third term?

PART 2 ★ ★ ★ The First Three Departments

The Department of State is concerned with how the United States gets along with other countries. This department sends people to places all over the world to represent the United States. *Ambassador* is the title given to a person who works for the State Department in a large foreign country. In a smaller country the title is *minister*. A *consul* is a representative sent to a foreign city. His or her office is called a *consulate*. A consulate can be found in almost every large foreign city in the world. Consuls and their staffs try to build up foreign trade and commerce for the United States. They also protect American citizens who travel, work, or own property in foreign countries.

The State Department is in charge of passports, which give permission to Americans to travel in foreign countries.

Department of the Treasury, Established in 1789

The Department of the Treasury collects taxes, borrows money when it is needed, and pays back the money. It prints and coins money. It is responsible for letting the president know about the financial standing of the United States. The Treasury Department makes sure that government money is spent as Congress has decided it should be spent.

Some important duties are taken care of by smaller units of the department:

- The Internal Revenue Service (IRS) collects taxes from individuals and from businesses.
- The Customs Service collects import taxes on goods that are brought in from foreign countries.
- The Secret Service protects the president, his family, and certain other people. It also safeguards against the use of counterfeit money.

Department of Justice, Established in 1870

The Department of Justice enforces federal laws. The head of the department is the Attorney General. All suits in the Supreme Court that involve the United States government are handled by the Justice Department. Several important agencies are within this department. When a federal law is violated, or broken, an investigation is carried out by the Federal Bureau of

Investigation (FBI), which is part of this department. This agency can arrest anyone who is accused of committing a crime against the federal government. The Immigration and Naturalization Service patrols the nation's borders to keep people from coming into the country illegally. The Bureau of Prisons is responsible for all persons convicted of federal crimes and sent to prison. It also runs all of the federal prisons and other institutions that house prisoners.

★**Activity B:** Number your paper from 1 to 9. For each description below, write the name of the correct department: *State, Treasury,* or *Justice.*
1. Prints money
2. Guards the nation's borders
3. Is concerned with how the United States deals with other countries
4. The Attorney General is head of this department
5. Lets the president know financial standing of the country
6. Helps protect Americans overseas
7. The Custom Service is part of this department
8. The Secret Service is part of this department
9. The Bureau of Prisons is part of this department

PART 3 ★★★ More Departments

WORDS TO KNOW
Conservation   *Minimum*
Environment

I t is the responsibility of the Department of the Interior to see that the United States' natural resources are used wisely. These resources include land, water, and minerals, as well as fish and wildlife. The Interior Department also looks after national parks and dams built by the federal government. The Interior Department has many divisions. Examples of these are the National Park Service, the Bureau of Indian Affairs, and the Fish and Wildlife Service.

Department of Agriculture, Established in 1862

The well-being of the United States and its people is dependent upon farmers in many ways. They have the important job of producing much of the food needed by the country. Many people have always felt that the federal government should help farmers in raising and selling crops.

Many agencies within the Agriculture Department aid farmers in planning and using the best farm methods. These agencies keep farmers informed about the market for livestock and crops. Such agencies also try to help farmers get the money they need to do their work. Two agencies that tend to these farm concerns are the Soil *Conservation* Service and the Farmers Home Administration that lends money to farmers.

The school lunch program, through the Department of Agriculture, provides states with funds to help furnish lunches to students from low income families. Food stamps are available to needy persons to assist them in purchasing food. The Department of Agriculture is responsible for inspecting and grading meat, poultry, and dairy products.

Department of Commerce, Established in 1903

Business and trade are important to the welfare of the United States. The Department of Commerce is concerned with business and trade in this country and in foreign countries. The department is made up of a number of agencies dealing with these matters. For instance, the Census Bureau reports on the population count in the United States. Inventors, people who create new products or ideas, are protected by the U.S. Patent Office. The U.S. Weather Bureau gathers information about storms, frosts, floods, and earthquakes. This information helps protect farmers, pilots, and sea-going vessels from the dangers that could be caused by violent weather.

The Department of Agriculture is not limited to helping only farmers. It also serves consumers by inspecting and grading meat, poultry, and dairy products.

American Ingenuity and the United States Patent Office

The early Americans were clever and ingenious people, and inventions were being made by the hundreds in the late 1700s. By 1790 the government opened the United States Patent Office in New York City to handle the flood of new inventions. Inventors applying for patents were required to submit models. Soon after it opened, the patent office had so many models that it was forced to move to a larger building. By 1836 there were 7,000 models on file — including self-propelled boats, steam engines, bridges, saw mills, threshing machines, and plows of all types. By 1870 there were 200,000 models and because so many models had been submitted, the government dropped the requirement that inventors submit models.

A patent is an official paper issued by the government. It is given to a person who has invented or discovered some new and useful machine, product, substance, or method. The patent refers to the right to control the manufacture and sale of the product for a certain number of years. All patents are still handled by the United States Patent Office, a part of the Department of Commerce. Individual states do not have the right to issue patents.

Department of Labor, Established in 1913

The Department of Labor offers many services to American workers. It sees that federal laws concerning labor are carried out, such as those on child labor and *minimum* wages. The Labor Department is made up of a number of agencies. The Bureau of Labor Statistics publishes information about the nation's work force, such as wages, prices, living conditions, and the size of the work force. The Occupational Safety and Health Administration (OSHA) sets standards for good work *environments*. The Employment and Training Administration helps people find jobs. Included in the Labor-Management Services Administration are the Office of Pensions and Welfare Services and the Office of Labor-Management Relations Services. These are only a few of the divisions within the Labor Department.

★Activity C: Number your paper from 1 to 8. Match the department or office in Part 1 to the correct description in Part 2.

Part 1, Department

1. Farmers Home Administration
2. Census Bureau
3. U.S. Patent Office
4. U.S. Weather Bureau
5. Department of Commerce
6. Department of the Interior
7. Department of Agriculture
8. Occupational Safety and Health Administration (OSHA)

Part 2, Description

a. Protects inventors
b. Lends money to farmers
c. Gathers information about storms, earthquakes, and floods
d. Concerned with business and trade
e. Oversees the use of natural resources
f. Reports population count
g. Helps farmers in raising and selling crops
h. Sets standards for good work environment

PART 4 ★ ★ ★ Departments Established After 1945

WORDS TO KNOW

Civilian   *Prosper*
Consumers   *Statistics*

In 1947 Congress decided to combine the War Department and the Navy Department. The organization was called the Department of Defense. At that time all of the country's armed forces were put under the control of this one department. The Secretary of Defense is a *civilian,* and each branch of the armed forces has a Secretary who is also a civilian. There is a Secretary of the Army, Secretary of the Navy, and Secretary of the Air Force. None of these Secretaries have Cabinet rank. They advise the president about matters having to do with the military.

The Defense Department looks after many peacetime projects, too. An example is the branch of the Army called the Corps of Engineers. The Corps of Engineers helps with improving rivers and harbors and promoting flood control. Among the Defense Department's responsibilities are the schools that train officers for military service. They are the Naval Academy at Annapolis, Maryland; the Military Academy at West Point, New

York; and the Air Force Academy at Colorado Springs, Colorado.

Department of Housing and Urban Development, Established in 1965

As the cities in the United States grew, so did their problems. Cities experienced an increase in the number of low income families who lived there. The cities needed help in providing homes and community development, in repairing buildings, and in protecting *consumers*. The Department of Housing and Urban Development was established to help the cities. It deals with all types of problems, including aid in financing housing, promoting water conservation, and protection against air pollution.

Department of Transportation, Established in 1966

For a nation to *prosper* the easy movement of goods and services from place to place is important. The citizens of a country also need to travel easily. As the United States' population expanded, more highways, railroads, airports, and waterways were needed. The Transportation Department was created to make all methods of travel more economical and efficient. It also sets safety standards for vehicles.

The Coast Guard is operated by the Department of Transportation in peacetime. The Coast Guard protects life and property at sea. It also enforces federal maritime, or shipping, laws.

Department of Energy, Established in 1977

The Department of Energy came into being to find and protect sources of energy such as water power, oil, and natural gas. It also regulates the sale of fuel and electricity.

Nuclear power plants such as Calvert Cliffs located in Maryland are capable of producing great amounts of energy at lower costs than fossil fuel plants, but their use remains limited because of concern over radioactive leaks.

The United States has long depended on other countries for petroleum. Government officials decided that the United States needed to protect its decreasing supplies of oil. Federal programs were set up to experiment with new ways to produce energy. Solar energy, or energy from the sun, is being used in some homes and industries. Nuclear power is another energy source. Its use has been limited because of the concern of many people who fear radioactive leaks. Other ways to produce power for automobiles are also being investigated. The Department of Energy works to meet the country's energy needs.

Department of Health and Human Services, Established in 1979

The Department of Health and Human Services is second in size only to the Defense Department. It was formerly part of the Department of Health, Education, and Welfare, established in 1953. In 1979 it was split into the Department of Health and Human Services and the Department of Education. Health and Human Services handles the social welfare programs of our country.

An agency within this department, the Social Security Administration, is probably the best known of its services. Health care for the elderly is handled by the Social Security Administration. This service is called Medicare. Other services included in this department are aid to the handicapped, research into the treatment and cures for diseases, and the enforcement of laws concerning pure food, drugs, and cosmetics.

Department of Education, Established in 1979

From 1953 to 1979, educational matters were looked after by the Department of Health, Education, and Welfare. Since that time the Department of Education has been concerned with the well-being of the country's educational systems. It offers financial help for all levels and types of education. Elementary schools, high schools, colleges, and educational programs for the handicapped, disadvantaged, and the gifted may receive aid from this department. *Statistics* about schools are gathered and published. The department encourages experimental programs to improve education.

Department of Veterans Affairs Established in 1988

From 1930 until 1988, the Veterans Administration (VA) provided services to ex-military personnel and their families. The VA services included health care and educational assistance programs. The VA operated about 170 veterans hospitals. It was also responsible for more than 100 national cemeteries. In 1988, the VA became an executive department of the government. It was renamed the Department of Veterans Affairs. The department took over all of the responsibilities of the VA.

★Activity D: Number your paper from 1 to 8. Write the word that completes each sentence below.

urban   grown
Defense   Medicare
Transportation   Education
energy   agencies

1. In recent years the number of low income families in the cities has ___.

2. The military is the main concern of the Department of ___.

3. The Social Security Administration is one of the ___ within the Department of Health and Human Services.

4. Housing and Urban Development deals with all kinds of ___ problems.

5. The Department of ___ sets standards for vehicle safety.

6. The Department of Energy has set up programs to find new ways to produce ___.

7. The Department of Health and Human Service provides health care to the elderly through ___.

8. All the country's schools receive aid from the Department of ___.

C H A P T E R ★ S U M M A R Y

The Constitution states that the president should have help to run the country successfully. When the United States was new, three departments were set up to help George Washington, the country's first president. They were the Departments of State, War, and the Treasury. Secretaries who headed these departments were the first three members of what was to become the president's Cabinet. The Cabinet is made up of the heads of the executive departments. Today there are fourteen such departments.

To protect the United States' natural resources, the Interior Department was set up in 1849. The Department of Agriculture began in 1862 to help farmers. In 1870 the Justice Department was established to see that federal laws were obeyed.

The Department of Commerce's main concern is business and trade between foreign countries and the United States. It was established in 1903. Ten years later, in 1913, the Department of Labor was established to look after the welfare of American workers.

The Defense Department was an outgrowth of the Departments of War and Navy. It was established in 1947, after World War II. All of the armed forces are under its control.

In more recent years five departments have come into existence. The Department of Housing and Urban Development was set up in 1965 to help with housing and other problems of big cities. In 1966 the Department of Transportation was created to help with our country's highways, railroads, airports, and waterways. The Department of Energy was established in 1977 to protect our sources of energy and to see that those sources are used wisely.

In 1979 the Department of Health and Human Services was established. It handles the social welfare programs. The newest of the departments is the Department of Education which is concerned with the well-being of schools the country's educational system. In 1988 the Department of Veterans Affairs took over the responsibilities of the Veterans Administration.

C H A P T E R ★ R E V I E W

Comprehension:
Recalling the Facts
Directions: Number your paper from 1 to 10. Write the answers.

1. What are the names of the fourteen executive departments?
2. What were the first three departments to be established?
3. Which department collects taxes?
4. Which department is concerned with the quality of schools?
5. Which department looks after community development projects?
6. Which department is in charge of the military?
7. To which department does the FBI belong?
8. Which department runs the National Park Service?
9. Which department sends ambassadors to foreign countries?
10. Which department does research on growing crops?

Comprehension:
Understanding Main Ideas
Directions: Write the answers to the following questions using complete sentences.

1. Today there are fourteen executive departments to aid the President. What important group is made up of the heads of these departments?
2. The Department of State sends people worldwide to represent our government. What are the three different types of representatives and whom do they serve?
3. What are three natural resources that are the responsibility of the Department of the Interior?
4. What important department was established in 1913? Name three services provided by this department.
5. Give three reasons why the Department of Housing and Urban Development was set up in 1956.

Critical Thinking:
Writing Your Opinion
1. Why do you think the three departments established in the 1970s were necessary? Which of these do you think is the most important and why?
2. Do you think it is necessary to have a separate department to take care of education? Give reasons for your answer.

CHAPTER
SEVEN

★ ★ ★

The Independent Agencies

How Independent Agencies Work

W O R D S   T O   K N O W

Communication	*Misuse*
Free enterprise	*Nuclear*
Frequency	*Radioactive material*
Interstate	*Regulate*

Independent agencies are created by Congress. They have definite powers to deal with certain matters which no other department of government handles. Even though they are spoken of as "independent," these agencies do not stand completely alone. They are involved with the three branches of the government. The president, head of the executive branch, appoints the heads of the agencies. In the legislative branch, the Senate must approve the president's appointments and Congress must approve the budgets of the agencies. Also, the agencies must file reports with Congress once or twice a year. Sometimes the judicial branch reviews the decisions the other branches make concerning the independent agencies.

The First Independent Agency

In the 1880s some of the problems that citizens and businesses were having could not be handled by the three branches of government. For example, farmers needed to use the railroads to transport animals and harvested crops. The farmers and the railroads could not agree about fair business practices, so Congress set up the *Interstate* Commerce Commission (ICC) to *regulate* the railroads. The ICC was the first independent agency.

Regulatory Agencies

Some of the agencies are regulatory. They have the authority to make rules about the activities they supervise. They also enforce their rules and regulations. Other agencies focus more on giving service to the public.

The Interstate Commerce Commission (1887)

The ICC was established to regulate the railroads. The railroads did not always treat the public fairly. Therefore, when the government stepped in, it saw to it that rates and schedules were planned for the public good. In this century the commission has overseen the commercial surface transportation between states. This includes all companies that move goods and passengers from state to state by trucks, trains, buses, or boats. These companies are required to get a permit from the ICC to operate. Interstate moving vans must have their rates approved by the ICC. They must also obey the ICC safety rules about lights, brakes, and rest stops.

The Federal Trade Commission (1914)

The Federal Trade Commission (FTC) was set up to prevent unfair trade practices and competition that would harm the *free enterprise* system in our country. The commission enforces laws that protect the public from such things as price fixing, false labeling, and advertising that makes untrue claims. The FTC also sees that products put on the market are safe for people to use. For instance, the commission makes sure that materials that burn easily and might harm people are not available for purchase. This agency also assures that labels on products are truthful so that a buyer knows what he or she is buying.

The Federal Communications Commission (1934)

The Federal Communications Commission does not control programs seen on television or heard on the radio. However, it does decide who can have a license to broadcast and what *frequencies* may be used. The FCC provides guidelines for the content of commercials. It also requires some public service broadcasts. It decides how much use can be made of the *communication* satellites (man-made objects that go around the earth). The commission sees to it that the nation's communication systems can take care of emergencies. For instance, in case of a natural disaster such as an earthquake or flood, communication is very important. This agency sees that good communication is available to the public.

The Environmental Protection Agency (1970)

The United States has become more and more densely populated, and the land has become more crowded with people and industry. When our country was younger, few people worried about overused land or cities becoming too crowded. There was always more land to move to. This is no longer true. People and industry can pollute air and water and *misuse* the land. The purpose of the Environmental Protection Agency (EPA) is to guard the country's environment. It enforces laws that Congress has passed to keep air and water clean and to prevent pollution.

The Nuclear Regulatory Commission (1974)

After World War II, this country became interested in the development of *nuclear* power for peaceful uses. Several agencies have served this purpose. In 1974 the Nuclear Regulatory Commission was established. The NRC exists to see that nuclear power plants operate safely. It gives permission for *radioactive material* to be stored or transported for civilian use. The commission studies ways to make working with nuclear material safer all the time. It may shut down any nuclear plant that is a danger to public health.

★**Activity A:** Number your paper from 1 to 10. Read each description. Decide which agency it fits. Write the name of that agency.
1. Gives licenses to radio and television stations.
2. Is responsible for safety at nuclear power plants.
3. Enforces laws that are meant to prevent pollution.
4. Approves rates used for interstate shipping.
5. Protects the consumer from untruthful advertising claims.
6. Gives permission for radioactive materials to be transported.
7. Was the first independent agency to be set up.
8. Sees that products on the market are safe to use.
9. Decides on how communications satellites may be used.
10. Carries out research on ways to keep the air clean.

THE FEDERAL BUREAUCRACY IS LIKE A LARGE PYRAMID

HIGHLIGHT STORY

★ ★ ★

The Executive Office of the president, the executive departments, and the many government independent agencies make up what is known as the federal bureaucracy. Think of the federal bureaucracy as a large pyramid. The bottom part, or foundation, is made up of many agencies which form the largest part of the federal government. Next come the executive departments, which are fewer in number. The attorney general or a secretary of the department serves in the president's cabinet. Next comes an even smaller group that makes up the Executive Office of the president. These individuals and agencies directly assist the president.

At the very top of the pyramid is the President of the United States, who has the highest position in the country. It is his responsibility to see that all parts of the government function as they should. It is important that each part of this pyramid does its job, if the government is to work well for the good of every citizen.

Review

Directions: On your own paper, answer the following questions with complete sentences.

1. What are the three major parts of the federal bureaucracy?
2. What makes up the foundation of the pyramid illustrating the federal bureaucracy?
3. Who represents each executive department?
4. What group directly assists the President?
5. Whose responsibility is it to see that the government functions as it should?

Pyramid diagram:

- President of the United States
- Executive Office
- State | Treasury
- Justice | Agriculture | Energy
- Defense | Transportation | Commerce | Labor
- Interior | Health and Human Services | Housing and Urban Development | Education | Veterans Administration

EXECUTIVE DEPARTMENTS

- Federal Trade Commission | Interstate Commerce Commission | Federal Communications Commission
- Environmental Protection Agency | Nuclear Regulatory Commission | National Aeronautics and Space Administration
- United States Postal Service | National Foundation on the Arts and Humanities | Federal Deposit Insurance Corporation | ACTION

And many others

INDEPENDENT AGENCIES

PART 2 ★ ★ ★ Some Service Agencies

WORDS TO KNOW

Aeronautics　　*Endowment*
Bankrupt　　　*Ghetto*
Civil servant　*Humanities*
Efficient　　　*Social work*

No government agency is better known to more people than the National *Aeronautics* and Space Administration, or NASA. Since it came into being in 1958, the American people have followed its many projects with great interest. It was established to help develop peaceful uses of outer space.

NASA has put satellites and astronauts into space and made it possible for men to walk on the moon. It did research for the creation of Skylab, which was used by scientists for experiments as it orbited high above the earth. Its space shuttle program has allowed people to go into space and return in the same vehicle. NASA's programs also helped in research for industry and medicine.

National Foundation on the Arts and the Humanities (1965)

Before the establishment of the National Foundation on the Arts and *Humanities* in 1965, the United States government had not done a great deal to encourage the development of arts and humanities. As Congress became aware of the importance of supporting the arts of the country, it set up this foundation. Two groups, the National *Endowment* for the Arts, and the National Endowment for the Humanities, do the work of the agency. These endowments make grants available to theaters, museums, music groups, talented individuals, and groups who best promote the arts

The space shuttle Atlantis *soars upward to begin its maiden flight on October 3, 1985.* Atlantis *is NASA's fourth space shuttle orbiter.*

and humanities in our country. The agency's purpose is to support the cultural life of the citizens.

Federal Deposit Insurance Corporation (1933)

During the Great Depression of the 1930s, many businesses and factories closed down. People lost their jobs. More banks failed during this time than at any other time in the history of the United States. Congress saw a need to protect people's money and to protect the banks from *bankruptcy*. It set up the Federal Deposit Insurance Corporation (FDIC). This agency pays people money, up to $100,000, that they may lose if a bank fails.

United States Postal Service (1971)

Until 1971 the United States Post Office was an executive department. Because this department usually lost money, the government saw a need to make the mail service more *efficient*, and the new service agency was created. The Postal Service is now run like a private business. It has a board headed by the postmaster general. A board of nine governors are appointed by the president. The governors appoint the postmaster general and the deputy postmaster. These appointments must be approved by the Senate. Postal workers are no longer *civil servants*. They have a union just as workers have in many other industries.

The Postal Service has certain powers to enforce laws concerning the mails. These laws make it illegal

The Pony Express

A short but exciting period in the development of the nation's mail service happened when the Pony Express was in operation. It started in April of 1860 and continued for about eighteen months. Brave young men on horseback carried the mail between the cities of St. Joseph, Missouri, and Sacramento, California. Then an ocean-going steamer would carry the mail to San Francisco, California. The system worked something like a relay race.

The riders would ride very fast — sometimes 25 miles an hour — from station to station. At the stations, which were about twelve miles apart, they would quickly pick up the mail and change horses. A rider would go about 75 miles before another rider would take over. This went on day and night, no matter how bad the weather might be.

The Pony Express proved to be faster than the stagecoach for delivering the mail. However, the telegraph, or wireless, method of sending messages came into use across the country in 1861. This was a much faster way of communicating with distant places. At this time the Pony Express came to an end. The people who invested in this mail delivery service lost their money.

to send certain items, such as firearms or liquor, through the mails. There is also a law against mailing lottery tickets, which are a form of gambling. If any such offense is found, the case is turned over to the Justice Department.

Even though the Postal Service is run like a business, if it loses money Congress must help pay for the service to the American people.

ACTION (1971)

ACTION is an agency that was set up as an organizer and supervisor of many volunteer programs sponsored by the government. The Peace Corps is the best known of these programs. A 1961 law established this program. The goal of the Peace Corps is to bring about peace and friendship between the United States and other countries. American citizens who wish to volunteer as teachers, farmers, engineers, or for other selected jobs are carefully chosen, trained, and sent to areas in foreign countries where their job skill is needed and requested.

Another well-known program is VISTA (Volunteers in Service to America). It serves needy citizens of our own country. VISTA workers are often found volunteering their time in such places as inner-city *ghettos*, Indian reservations, and migratory labor camps.

The success of these two programs inspired the creation of others. Through the Foster Grandparents Program, volunteer grandparents offer their time and interest to children who have little or no family. The Retired Senior Volunteer Program gives retired citizens the chance to use their work experience

Peace Corps volunteers teach their skills to people in developing countries to improve living conditions and promote peace.

to help others in their jobs. The Senior Companion Program brings together, on an individual basis, people who can help each other.

ACTION offers programs to young people. The University Year for ACTION lets students earn college credits while living and doing *social work* in poverty-stricken areas. The National Student Volunteer Program and the Youth Challenge Program are set up to train young people for volunteer service. These programs develop skills and allow the volunteers to serve where they are most needed.

★ **Activity B:** Complete the sentences by matching the sentence beginning in Part 1 with the correct sentence ending in Part 2.

Part 1, Beginning of Sentence

1. NASA was established...
2. NASA has put...
3. The Postal Service is run like a private business and is...
4. Skylab will be used by scientists...
5. The goal of the Peace Corps is...
6. The purpose of the National Foundation on the Arts and the Humanities is...
7. Endowments make grants available...
8. The greatest number of bank failures at one time...
9. The FDIC was set up to protect...
10. The insurance corporation Congress set up...

Part 2, Ending of Sentence

a. ...for experiments as it orbits above the Earth.
b. ...happened during the Great Depression of the 1930s.
c. ...to theaters, museums, music groups, and talented individuals.
d. ...to support the cultural life of the country for the enjoyment of the people.
e. ...guarantees to pay back money (up to $100,000) that depositors may lose when a bank fails.
f. ... people's money and the banks from bankruptcy.
g. ...headed by the postmaster general.
h. ...to bring about peace and friendship between the U. S. and other countries.
i. ...astronauts and satellites into space.
j. ...to help establish peaceful uses of space.

C H A P T E R ★ S U M M A R Y

Congress created the first independent government agency in 1887. An agency's purpose is to deal with some matter that is not being handled by any other part of the government. Even though the agencies are called independent, they are involved with the three branches of government: legislative, executive, and judicial.

There are dozens of independent agencies. Some are regulatory. They make rules and regulations about the activities they supervise. Other agencies perform services, either for the government or for the general public.

The regulatory agencies have many different concerns. One oversees the workings of surface interstate transportation. Another helps prevent unfair trade practices and competition. Other agencies supervise the nation's communication systems — radio and television — and enforce laws to protect the environment and help develop safe and peaceful uses of nuclear power.

The independent service agencies are also concerned with a number of matters. NASA is developing peaceful uses of space. Support for the arts — music, dance, theater, and museums — is made available by one service agency. Other agencies insure the money people deposit in banks, operate the nation's mail service, and supervise volunteer programs sponsored by the government.

National Aeronautics and
Space Administration

FEDERAL DEPOSIT INSURANCE CORPORATION

C H A P T E R ★ R E V I E W

Comprehension:
Identification
Directions: Number your paper from 1 to 10. Read each statement. Decide which type of agency is being described. Write *Regulatory* or *Service* next to each number.

1. Enforces laws intended to protect the environment.
2. Works to develop peaceful uses of space.
3. Supports the arts, including music, dance, and theater.
4. Has set up standards for buses that carry passengers to other states.
5. Insures the money that people put in banks.
6. Gives permission for a radio station to broadcast.
7. Sees that nuclear power plants are operated safely.
8. Supervises volunteer programs sponsored by the government.
9. Delivers mail.
10. Enforces rules about the kinds of labels that may be put on consumer goods.

Comprehension:
Understanding Main Ideas
Directions: Write the answers to the following questions using complete sentences.

1. How do the functions of the two types of agencies differ?
2. How does the Interstate Commerce Commission protect the public?
3. What information does the Federal Trade Commission require of labels on products?
4. What is the purpose of the National Foundation of the Arts and Humanities?
5. Name two volunteer programs that are supervised by Action. What is the purpose of these programs?

Critical Thinking:
Write Your Opinion

1. The government, through FDIC, protects people's investments in banks and also the banks themselves. This can be very expensive for the government. Do you think the FDIC will continue to operate as it has? Give reasons for your answer.
2. Do you think the work of the U. S. Postal Service has become more difficult over the years? Why?

CHAPTER
EIGHT

★ ★ ★

The Judicial Branch

PART 1 **Laws Protect**
★ ★ ★ **Rights of Citizens**

WORDS TO KNOW

Authority	*Innocent*
Customs	*Patent*
Disagreement	*Stationed*

Article III of the Constitution describes the third branch of the United States' government, the judicial branch. The judicial branch includes all of the federal courts.

All laws follow the ideals written in the Constitution. Every American citizen is responsible for knowing these laws. If a citizen does not obey a law, he or she can be arrested and tried. When this happens, the person still has certain rights. A person charged with violating the law has the right to a fair trial in a public court of law.

The Constitution says that a person is *innocent* until proven guilty. Only a court of law can decide that the person is guilty. Most cases are heard in lower courts, such as traffic courts, juvenile courts, and small claims courts. If the case involves a federal law, then the case is heard within the federal court system. The federal court system includes district courts, courts of appeals, and

Jury Trial

The Constitution, in the Sixth Amendment, provides that an accused person is guaranteed a speedy public trial by a jury in the state where the crime took place. He is to be told of the charge against him. He is entitled to have a lawyer to defend him.

The trial jury is made up of twelve persons who live in the community. They are chosen at random from lists of voters or taxpayers. They must decide, after hearing both sides of the case, whether a person is guilty or not guilty. All twelve members must agree on the guilt or innocence of the accused.

the Supreme Court. Other federal courts take care of taxes, *customs*, and *patents*.

Federal Courts Hear Certain Cases

State courts hear cases of persons who are charged with breaking the laws of the state. Most trials are heard in state courts. The federal courts hear only certain cases. The Constitution gives federal courts the *authority* to hear the following kinds of cases:

1. Of any person disobeying any part of the Constitution, including the amendments.
2. Of any person accused of breaking laws passed by Congress, such as tax laws, mail laws, banking laws, or military law.
3. Of a foreign nation suing the United States or a citizen of the United States.
4. Of any ambassador accused of breaking a law of the country in which he is *stationed*.
5. Of any crime committed on American ships at sea.
6. Of any crime committed on federal property.
7. Of any *disagreement* between states.
8. Of any lawsuit between citizens of different states.

Other Federal Courts and the Cases They Handle

Congress has set up a number of other federal courts to handle special cases. Some of these are:

1. Court of Claims—Hears cases involving money claims against the federal government. A decision in favor of the person bringing the suit usually results in a sum of money being given to that person.
2. Court of International Trade — Hears cases from individuals and businesses about tariffs and taxes collected by customs officials on imported goods.
3. Court of Customs and Patent Appeals — Hears cases appealed from Court of International Trade, from people applying for patents, and from people whose patent rights have been violated.
4. Territorial Courts—Hears cases of the people who live in territories of the United States overseas (Guam, the Virgin Islands, and Marianas. These courts work the same as the federal district courts.
5. Tax Court—Hears appeals concerning payment of federal taxes. Does not hear criminal cases, but settles arguments about the amount or type of tax.

District Courts

A district court is the place where federal cases are heard. Each state has at least one district court. Some larger states are divided into two or more districts. Each district has a district court. Several judges are assigned to each district court. District courts are the only federal courts which use juries.

District court judges are appointed for life. There is a Chief Judge for each district and one or more other judges. One duty of the judge is to explain to the jury the nature of the law that the defendant is accused of breaking. If the person is found guilty, then the judge decides on a sentence, or punishment.

District court judges hear a wide variety of cases that may include bank robbery, kidnapping, counterfeiting, or tax evasion (refusing to pay taxes).

★**Activity A:** Number your paper from 1 to 8. Choose the correct ending for each sentence from the two endings given. Write the letter you choose next to each number.

1. A district court is the only federal court
   (a) in which a jury trial is held.
   (b) that is in the federal court system.
2. District courts are found
   (a) in every state.
   (b) only in the larger states.
3. An accused person is guaranteed a speedy public trial
   (a) in the state where the crime took place.
   (b) in Washington, D.C.
4. An accused person must be told
   (a) nothing about the charge against him.
   (b) about the charge against him.
5. The trial jury is made up of
   (a) twelve persons who live in the community.
   (b) people chosen by the accused.
6. The decision as to whether a person is guilty or not must be agreed upon by
   (a) all twelve members of the jury.
   (b) a majority of the jury members.
7. The district court judge explains to the jury
   (a) the law involved in the case.
   (b) why the accused person is guilty or not guilty.
8. The sentence given to a person found guilty of a crime is decided by the
   (a) jury.
   (b) judge.

PART 2 ★ ★ ★ United States Court of Appeals

WORDS TO KNOW

Appeal   *Review*
Final

I f an accused person feels that his trial was unfair in a district court, he may *appeal* his case, or ask a higher court to *review* his case. This review would then take place in a court of appeals.

The United States Court of Appeals was set up by Congress in 1891. This court handles almost every appeal from the district courts. The nation is divided into twelve large judicial areas known as circuits. In each circuit there is a United States Court of Appeals. The number of judges varies from circuit to circuit.

When a Court of Appeals gets a case to review, the judges study the history of the case. At least three judges take part in the review. They do not decide whether the person is guilty or innocent. There is no jury trial. The reason for review is largely based upon the question of legal procedures or interpretation of the law. The judges listen to the lawyers from each side. They carefully check written records from the district court. When all the facts are presented, the three judges vote. If the judges decide that justice was not done and the trial was not fair, the case is sent back to the district court for a new trial. Or, the judges may decide that justice was done. Then the verdict that was reached by the district court will stand firm. This decision made by the court of appeals is *final* in most cases.

★Activity B: Number your paper from 1 to 5. Choose the best word to complete each sentence. Write the correct word next to each number.

1. The United States Court of Appeals were set up by the (Constitution, Congress, Senate) in 1891.

2. Every circuit has a United States Court of Appeals that reviews decisions made in (higher courts, state courts, district courts).

3. The judges in the Court of Appeals listen to arguments presented by the (accused, judges, lawyers) from each side.

4. A case may be sent back to a district court for a new trial if the judges decide that (justice, argument, an appeal) was not done.

5. If the Court of Appeals decides that justice was done, the (judge, argument, decision) of the district court will stand.

PART 3 ★ ★ ★ The Supreme Court

W O R D S   T O   K N O W

Apportion   *Segregate*
Challenge

The Supreme Court of the United States is the highest court in the nation. Its decisions are final and cannot be appealed. In most instances the Supreme Court receives cases after they have passed through a district court and a court of appeals. Someone has to *challenge* the law involved in the case before the case can come to the Supreme Court. The Supreme Court decides whether or not it will review the case. Once it decides to hear the case, the Court then makes a decision about the law involved. It rules whether or not the law is unconstitutional. If the intent of the law is ruled unconstitutional, it means that the law has gone against the Constitution.

There are nine justices, or judges, on the Supreme Court, including a chief justice and eight associate justices. Congress has the power to change this number and has done so several times in history. The total number of nine justices was determined in 1869. The Supreme Court justices are appointed by the president for life. These appointments must be approved by the Senate. A justice may serve as long as he or she feels able to do so. Justices may resign at any time. If they are accused of wrongdoing, they may be impeached, or brought to trial by the Congress.

Supreme Court Sessions

The Supreme Court works in Washington, D.C. Its term, or period of work, begins the first Monday in October each year and continues

After approval from the Senate, President Bush appointed Justice Souter to serve on the Supreme Court in 1990.

until late June. For the first two weeks, the justices hold public sessions, or sittings. All justices are present and listen to the facts of each case. The chief justice sits in the middle of the group. Lawyers from both sides are given a limited amount of time to explain their case. The justices may question the lawyers.

For the next two weeks, the justices study the facts of the case presented, and the lawyers provide them with briefs (written statements about the case). This period of study is called a recess. Throughout the rest of the term, the justices follow this pattern of sitting and recesses.

The decisions made in the Supreme Court are reached by a majority vote of the nine justices. Six justices must be present to call for a vote. After the court has voted, it writes an opinion. This is a carefully worded statement that explains why the decision was made. The writing of an opinion takes a long time. Both the opinions for and against the decision are written down. These opinions are then published in a series of books titled *United States Reports*.

Washington, D.C., is home to the Supreme Court. The nine justices of the highest court in the United States protect the rights of citizens by deciding whether or not the laws are constitutional.

Is the Supreme Court Too Powerful?

The decisions of the Supreme Court are final. Early in the history of our country, Thomas Jefferson and some other Americans did not agree with all the decisions the Supreme Court made. They thought the Supreme Court had become too powerful because it could decide that a law was unconstitutional. However, not all Americans felt the way Jefferson and others did. Many people thought that these rulings were good because laws were improved while rights were protected. They could see that the changes kept laws up-to-date.

CHIEF JUSTICE JOHN MARSHALL AND HIS INFLUENCE

In 1801 President Adams appointed John Marshall as chief justice. He remained in this role as head of the Supreme Court for 34 years. During his term the Court made decisions in more than 500 cases. He helped establish the Supreme Court as a powerful influence for justice. Before his term the Supreme Court was poorly respected. It was difficult to get men to serve as justices.

Marshall's decisions established three basic ideals that are followed today by the Supreme Court. They are as follows:

1. The Supreme Court does have the power to declare a law unconstitutional. A law that goes against the Constitution must be changed.
2. The Supreme Court may set aside (overrule) state laws if they are against the Constitution.
3. The Supreme Court may reverse (change) the decisions of any court, even state courts.

Through the years these principles, or ideals, followed by the Supreme Court mean that the Court has the final word in deciding what the Constitution means. The Supreme Court interprets, or explains, the Constitution for us.

Review

Directions: On your own paper, answer the following questions in complete sentences.

1. How long did John Marshall remain Chief Justice of the Supreme Court?
2. How did people feel about the Supreme Court before 1801?
3. What happens to a law that is declared unconstitutional by the Supreme Court?
4. How does the Supreme Court handle state laws that go against the Constitution?
5. Why is the Supreme Court so important in regards to the Constitution?

In spite of the disagreements among officials since Jefferson's time, the Supreme Court has continued to use its power to change laws.

Supreme Court Decisions Can Lead to Changes in the Constitution

In the past some Supreme Court decisions have even brought about changes in the Constitution. For example, the Constitution states in Article I, Section 9 that direct taxes must be *apportioned* according to the population of each state. This means that taxes must come equally from every state. In 1895 the Supreme Court ruled that income taxes were unconstitutional because they did not come evenly from each state. As a result of this decision, the Sixteenth Amendment was written, passed by all the states, and added to the Constitution. It stated that Congress was allowed to tax incomes without apportionment among the states.

The Supreme Court May Change Its Mind

The Supreme Court can make a decision that is exactly the opposite of an earlier decision. This happened with the issue of *segregated* schools (separate schools for black and white children). In the 1880s many southern states set up separate schools for blacks and whites. Some Americans declared that these segregated schools were unequal, and that was against the Fourteenth Amendment. The Fourteenth Amendment states in part:

"...Nor shall any state deprive any person of life, liberty, or property, without due process of law; nor deny to any person within its jurisdiction the equal protection of the laws."

In 1896 a case called for the end of segregated schools because some people said these schools did not give equal education to all students. The Supreme Court was asked to make a decision whether or not these schools violated the intent of the Constitution. The Court ruled in favor of segregated schools, saying that they were equal even though they were separate. The Court was saying that the schools did not go against the Constitution and therefore could remain segregated.

In 1954 another case concerning segregated schools came before the Supreme Court. The National Association for the Advancement of Colored People (NAACP) sued the Board of Education of Topeka, Kansas. The NAACP argued that the separate schools operating in Topeka were illegal. They claimed that the white schools were better equipped and not equal to the black schools. The NAACP said that this went against the Fourteenth Amendment. This time the Supreme Court ruled that the segregated schools were illegal because they went against the idea of equality stated in the Fourteenth Amendment. The Court said the schools should be desegregated immediately. The Supreme Court had changed its mind.

Because of the decision in the case concerning the schools of Topeka, segregated public schools became illegal. Although the Supreme Court said segregation in schools must be stopped, many American schools remained segregated. The Court's decision was not liked by many, and some Americans refused to accept it. Finally, in the 1960s, laws approving segregation were removed one by one. Laws supporting black voting rights were passed. The civil rights of all citizens were beginning to be enforced in the United States.

★Activity C: Number your paper from 1 to 8. From the list of words, select the correct word for each blank. Write the word beside the correct number.

opposite	highest
unconstitutional	review
eight	opinion
Senate	life

1. The Supreme Court is the ___ court in the nation.
2. The Supreme Court may decide whether or not to ___ a case.
3. The Supreme Court may decide that a law is ___.
4. There are ___ associate justices on the Supreme Court.
5. The justices are appointed for a ___ term.
6. An appointment of a Supreme Court justice must be approved by the ___.
7. An ___ is a carefully worded statement that explains why a decision was made.
8. Sometimes the Supreme Court can make a decision that is the ___ of an earlier decision.

C H A P T E R ★ S U M M A R Y

In this chapter you learned about the judicial branch, which is the third part of the federal government. It includes all the federal courts and judges. If people are accused of breaking the law in the United States, the Constitution says that they are innocent until proven guilty. Each case is tried in a court of law. If the case involves a federal law, then it is tried within the federal court system.

There are three main courts in the federal court system: district courts, the Courts of Appeals, and the Supreme Court. District courts are located in every state and hold jury trials. The decision of the district court can be questioned, or appealed, in a Court of Appeals. The case does not receive another jury trial in this court, but is reviewed by the judges. From the Court of Appeals, a case may be taken to the Supreme Court if the Supreme Court agrees to hear it.

The Supreme Court is the only court in the country that can decide which cases it will hear. The decision of the Supreme Court is final. The Supreme Court has the power to decide if the law involved in a case it hears is constitutional. If the justices decide that it is unconstitutional, then the law has no force and must be changed. The Supreme Court alone has the power to interpret, or explain, the Constitution for the citizens of our country. Sometimes the Supreme Court changes its mind and reverses an earlier decision, as it did with public school segregation.

The Congress also has set up a number of other special federal courts. There is a court to handle appeals about taxes. Another court hears cases from individuals and businesses who make property or money claims against the federal government. Still other courts handle cases involving customs laws and patent appeals and violations.

All of the courts mentioned have judges who are appointed by the government. The nine Supreme Court justices, or judges, are the most important and have the most power. The head of these justices is the chief justice of the United States.

C H A P T E R ★ R E V I E W

Comprehension:
Vocabulary

Directions: Number your paper from 1 to 10. From the list below, select the word that correctly completes each sentence. Write the correct word beside each number.

final	*nine*
judges	*Constitution*
innocent	*reversed*
district	*appealed*
three	*chooses*

1. There are ___ levels of federal courts.
2. A person in our country is ___ until proven guilty by a court of law.
3. The only federal courts that hold jury trials are ___ courts.
4. A decision from a district court may be ___.
5. At least three ___ review a case brought to a Court of Appeals.
6. The Supreme Court is the highest court in the nation, and its decisions are ___.
7. There are ___ justices serving on the Supreme Court, and they are all appointed by the president.
8. The Supreme Court ___ which cases it will hear.
9. The Supreme Court has ___, or changed, its decisions from time to time.
10. Supreme Court decisions have sometimes brought about changes in the ___ itself.

Comprehension:
Understanding Main Ideas

Directions: Write the answers to the following questions using complete sentences.

1. Federal courts hear cases of persons accused of breaking laws passed by Congress. What are these laws?
2. How many circuits include a United States Court of Appeals?
3. Why would a person go to an appeals court?
4. What is included in an opinion, the written statement of the Supreme Court?
5. In what year did the Supreme Court decide that segregated schools were illegal?

Critical Thinking:
Writing Your Opinion

1. Do you think the Supreme Court should be allowed to change its mind and reverse earlier decisions it has made? Give reasons for your decision.
2. If you were asked to serve on a jury, would you look forward to the experience or try to be excused from the responsibility? Why?

CHAPTER NINE

State Government

WORDS TO KNOW

Admit   *Statehood*
Eligible   *Treaty*
Independent

Thirteen states existed as separate governments before the federal government was formed. In 1787 the Constitution was written by the original states to give certain powers to the federal government. All other powers were kept by the states. The new federal government was modeled after the government of the original states. The thirty-seven states that were admitted later were modeled after the federal government.

The name, "United States of America," means a group of states joined by the rule of the federal government in Washington, D.C. The individual states share the same goals and ideals. Although the fifty state governments are similar in many ways, each state has some rules which are different because of its location, population, and local industry. Each state also grants smaller local areas within the state the power to rule themselves.

In 1788, when the Constitution went into effect, the country was made up of thirteen states. By 1959, when Alaska and Hawaii became states, the country had grown to fifty states. Most states entered the country before 1900. Only five states were admitted after 1900.

The Last Five States Admitted		
STATE	**YEAR ADMITTED**	**NUMBER**
Oklahoma	1907	Forty-sixth
New Mexico	1912	Forty-seventh
Arizona	1912	Forty-eighth
Alaska	1959	Forty-ninth
Hawaii	1959	Fiftieth

Congress Has Power to Admit States

The United States Constitution gives Congress the power to *admit* states. Over the years Congress has acted thirty-seven times to admit new states to the country. Some states were formed by dividing old states. Maine was once a part of Massachusetts. Texas was an *independent* republic before it joined the country in 1845. Other states were formed from land the United States had bought or had gained by wars and *treaties* with other countries.

Most States Began as Territories

The thirteen original colonies joined together to form the United States when they approved the Constitution. Most of the other states were territories first. A territory is an area that has to follow the rules and laws of the government.

Officials were appointed by Congress to rule the territories. If a territory wanted to become a state, it had to petition, or ask, Congress for *statehood*. The territory needed to have at least five thousand male voters to elect its lawmaking body. When the entire population of the territory reached sixty thousand voters, it was *eligible* to become a state.

If Congress agreed that a territory was ready to become a state, it passed a special act. This act, called an Enabling Act, asked the people of the territory to write a state constitution. When the new state constitution was approved by the people of the territory and the United States Congress, this new state was admitted to the United States.

★Activity A: Number your paper from 1 to 7. Choose the word to complete each sentence. Write this word next to the number.

1. The United States is a group of (states, countries) joined by the rule of a federal government.
2. Alaska and Hawaii became states in (1900, 1959).
3. Most states in the United States began as (republics, territories).
4. The territories were governed by officials appointed by the (Constitution, Congress).
5. A territory needed sixty thousand (people, voters) before it could ask Congress for statehood.
6. A state (constitution, Congress) had to be written and approved before statehood was granted.
7. The state constitution had to be approved by the people of the territory and by the (Congress, president).

"SOONERS" HELPED BUILD OKLAHOMA INTO A STATE

HIGHLIGHT STORY

★ ★ ★

In 1889 Oklahoma was a western district. President Harrison announced that free homesteads of 160 acres would be available "at and after the hour of 12 o'clock noon, on the 22nd day of April" in the district of Oklahoma. This set off a wild rush toward the district. The army set up patrols along the border to guard against people staking their claims before the proper time. Soon people camped at the borders to wait, and others were on their way. All roads leading to the area were jammed with wagons, carts, and men and women on horseback. By the morning of April 22nd, there were about 200,000 people waiting for the signal to go. At the sound of a shot fired at exactly 12 noon, the stampede began. But, even the fastest riders discovered that much of the district was already claimed. They were not "soon" enough. In spite of all precautions, some "sooners" had managed to slip past the patrols at the borders and stake their claims before the official time. Within a few hours of 12 noon on the first day, every bit of the Oklahoma land was claimed. Thousands of disappointed settlers had to go back home along the same roads they had come.

In 1890 Oklahoma had enough people to become a territory. Soon after, other areas in the territory were opened to homesteaders, and in 1907 Oklahoma was admitted as the 46th state.

Review

Directions: Answer the following questions in complete sentences on your own paper.

1. What had the government done to encourage people to come and settle in the district of Oklahoma?
2. What had the government done to prevent people from staking their claims too early?
3. Why were some people disappointed on April 22, 1889?
4. How long did it take, after the land rush, for Oklahoma to become a state?
5. What president was responsible for the land rush in the district of Oklahoma?

PART 2 ★ ★ ★ Each State Has Its Own Constitution

W O R D S   T O   K N O W

Borough   *Reserved*
Document

The original thirteen colonies wrote their constitutions after the Declaration of Independence was written. Until that time the colonies were ruled by charters. Charters were *documents* given by England that allowed each colony to govern itself. As each state was admitted to the United States, it wrote its own constitution.

Most state constitutions are longer and more detailed than the United States Constitution. One reason for this is that people have always been afraid of giving too much power to a government. In order to prevent the misuse of power by the state government, many rules and regulations were put in the state constitution.

Amendments to state constitutions are often made that add to their length. Some of the older constitutions still have laws and regulations that no longer apply, but which have never been removed.

Because the state constitutions were modeled after the United States Constitution, the same basic ideals, or guidelines, were used. These basic principles are:

1. **Popular sovereignty**
   People control their government because they elect the leaders.

2. **Separation of powers**
   Each of the three branches of state government has separate and definite powers. This keeps any one branch from becoming too powerful.

3. **Checks and balances**
   Each branch can check on the work of another branch. Certain actions and decisions must sometimes be approved by other branches. For example, judges appointed by the executive branch must be approved by the legislature.

4. **Limited government**
   State and federal officials are not above the law. They must obey the Constitution. The government must never do anything that takes away from an individual's basic freedoms as explained in the Bill of Rights.

What State Constitutions Contain

The special needs of each state require that state constitutions be different in some ways. They may contain many laws to take care of these special needs. However, all state constitutions, no matter how large or small, are similar in certain ways. Each explains how the state government is to be set up and run. All state constitutions contain the following parts:

1. Preamble — A statement of goals and purposes.
2. Bill of Rights — A list of freedoms and rights given to each citizen.
3. Organization of the Government — Lists the duties of the three branches of government.
4. Election Rules — Explains how to handle elections and how to qualifiy for each office.
5. Other Regulations — Gives guidelines for providing state education, keeping order, building and caring for highways and roads, operating businesses, and collecting taxes.
6. Process for Making Amendments — Explains ways to change or amend the laws and regulations that rule the state.
7. Amendments — The actual changes that have been made to the state constitution.

States Have Reserved and Shared Powers

The states have certain powers that the federal government does not have. These are called *reserved* powers. The states reserved, or kept,

these powers for themselves when they wrote and approved the United States Constitution.

Reserved Powers of the States
- To establish local governments.
- To regulate trade within the state.
- To run elections.
- To establish schools.
- To license professional workers, such as doctors and lawyers.
- To protect the lives and property of the people.

States also share responsibilities with the federal government. These shared powers mean that both the state and federal government can do some things at their own levels. For example, both groups collect taxes. People are usually required to pay taxes to both the state and federal governments.

Powers Shared by States and the Federal Government
- To make laws.
- To enforce laws.
- To establish courts.
- To collect taxes.
- To borrow money.
- To spend money for the health and welfare of people.
- To establish banks.

State Government Affects the Daily Lives of People

Most laws and rules that affect the daily lives of people are made by state governments. Many of the laws that tell which actions are crimes are decided by the state. State laws also control guidelines for education, driving an automobile, and marriage.

State laws also explain how local governments are set up and operated. Local governments can be divided between county, city, township, village, or *borough*. State law even decides how large school districts will be, although these districts are run by their own officials.

★**Activity B:** Number your paper from 1 to 10. Choose the correct ending for each sentence from the two given. Write the letter of that ending by the number.

1. The United States Constitution and the state constitutions were written
   (a) using the same basic principles as guidelines.
   (b) with different ideals or principles.

2. Separation of powers means that
   (a) all power is given to one branch of government.
   (b) power is divided among three branches of government.

3. The principle of popular sovereignty means people are in charge of their government because
   (a) they elect the leaders.
   (b) they sometimes do not have to obey the law.

4. The goals and ideals of a constitution are written in the
   (a) amendments.
   (b) preamble.

5. All state constitutions contain election rules which tell how
   (a) education is to be managed.
   (b) elections should be run, and lists the qualifications of candidates.

6. The list of rights and freedoms is called the
   (a) preamble.
   (b) bill of rights.
7. All state governments have
   (a) three branches — legislative, executive, and judicial.
   (b) only two branches to carry out the duties.
8. All state constitutions may be amended, which means that
   (a) they may be changed or added to.
   (b) they have no way of being changed.
9. The principle of checks and balances means that
   (a) the branches of government have nothing to do with each other.
   (b) each branch may check on the work of the other branches.
10. State and federal officials
    (a) must always obey the law.
    (b) can take away some basic rights.

PART 3 ★ ★ ★ State Governments Need Money

W O R D S   T O   K N O W
Percentage   *Grant*

Most state governments have yearly budgets of more than a billion dollars. Such large amounts are needed because states provide many services for their citizens.

In order to maintain such large budgets, states must get funding from many sources. Among those sources are personal income taxes, sales taxes, federal funds, and gasoline taxes. The graph below shows where one state gets its money.

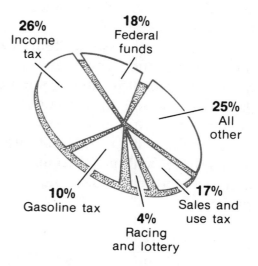

26%
Income tax

18%
Federal funds

25%
All other

10%
Gasoline tax

4%
Racing and lottery

17%
Sales and use tax

Where One State's Money Comes From

Personal Income Tax

Most states collect a personal income tax from their citizens. A personal income tax is what state residents must pay on the money they earn from their job. If citizens live in one state and work in another, they pay income tax in the state where they work. Income taxes usually account for about twenty-five percent of the total money needed for a state to operate.

Sales Tax

The second largest source of income for many states is their sales tax. A sales tax is a set *percentage* of money that people pay on goods or services they buy. Sales taxes vary from state to state.

In most states, some items like milk, bread, and other necessities are not taxed. Other items, such as gasoline, cigarettes, and alcoholic beverages, have special taxes. Some states charge a tax on restaurant meals, hotel and motel rooms, and admission to theaters and amusement parks.

Federal Funds

Some of the money the federal government collects in taxes is used to aid the states. The amount of federal funds varies from state to state and from year to year. In some states federal funds might make up one-fifth of the budget. Federal support to a state is often given as a *grant*. Such grants must, by law, be used in certain ways. The state must follow guidelines set by the federal government. For example, a federal grant for state education must follow rules set by the national government that do not permit discrimination. Discrimination is unfair treatment of any person or group of individuals because of their race, beliefs, sex, or age. Buildings or highways built with federal money must follow certain requirements set by the national government.

Other Taxes and Fees

In addition to personal income tax, sales tax, and federal funds, other fees are collected by the state. Citizens pay for driver's licenses and for automobile registration and tags. There are fees for recording certain official papers, such as titles to property. Most businesses and many professionals pay fees to be licensed to perform their work. Some states charge tolls for using certain roads and bridges. Some states permit racing or lotteries and receive a percentage of the money that is taken in from these activities.

★Activity C: Answer each of the questions using complete sentences.

1. Name three sources of income for a state.
2. What is a sales tax?
3. What is discrimination?
4. How does the federal government sometimes give financial aid to a state?
5. How do some states get additional money other than taxes?

States and Money

W O R D S T O K N O W

Correctional   Regulation

In most states the largest part of the budget is spent on public education. Much of the money is used to operate the state colleges and universities. Some money pays for new school buildings, education for the handicapped, and education for very young children. Only a small portion of money goes to elementary and secondary schools because they are operated mainly on local tax money.

Although the state sets some rules for schools, most of the decisions are made by local school officials. The state may decide how many days schools should be in session each year. The state also requires teachers to meet certain educational standards.

Building and maintaining highways, roads, and bridges take up fifteen to twenty percent of their yearly budgets for many states. Money is also provided by the states to train the unemployed for new jobs. They offer assistance to needy and disabled people.

Many states have state hospitals that offer special kinds of treatment.

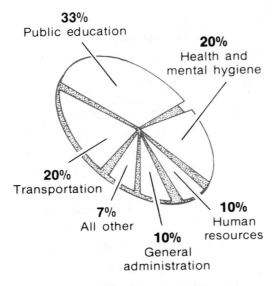

33%
Public education

20%
Health and
mental hygiene

20%
Transportation

7%
All other

10%
General
administration

10%
Human
resources

How One State's Money
Is Spent

States also help pay the costs of certain patients in nursing homes. States often have guidelines for hospitals and doctors to follow. There are also guidelines for the sale of medicine. Restaurants must follow certain health *regulations* in the handling of food. School children are required to have health exams. The state pays to see that its guidelines are followed.

Other Expenses

The states have many other expenses.

1. General administration — This expense includes salaries and benefits for state employees and the maintenance of office buildings and equipment.

2. State police force — This group provides protection and law enforcement. It assists other organizations in crime prevention.

3. Courts and prisons — A series of courts handles civil and criminal cases. States usually have several *correctional* institutions and prisons.

4. National guard — This citizens' militia provides local military protection in emergencies. It gives assistance during disasters.

5. Regulatory agencies — These groups provide rules for banks, insurance companies, and public utilities, such as telephone, gas, and electric companies. The state also watches over the safety standards and working conditions in factories, stores, and mines.

6. Park land — States buy land to be used for parks. They spend money to improve existing parks.

State government requires billions of dollars each year and employs thousands of citizens. Strong state governments with careful planning provide programs that their citizens need.

★**Activity D:** Complete the following statements with the correct word. Write the word on your own paper.

1. The largest part of a state's budget is spent on ___.
2. Much of the state's education budget is spent on ___ and ___.
3. About 20 percent of a state's budget is spent on ___.
4. The citizen's militia that gives assistance during disasters is called the ___ ___.
5. States buy land to provide ___ for recreation.

PART 5 ★ ★ ★ # The Legislative Branch

WORDS TO KNOW

Legislators   *Pro tempore*

The legislative branch of each state has a lawmaking body that works nearly the same as the Congress, the lawmaking body of the federal government. The main duty of this lawmaking body is to pass laws. In most states the name for this group is the Legislature. Some states use names such as General Assembly or Legislative Assembly. The name General Court is used by the states of Massachusetts and New Hampshire.

Two Houses

Just like the Congress, state legislatures have two houses — the Senate and the House of Representatives. The state of Nebraska is the exception. It has only one house in its legislature. While no state has a legislature as large as Congress, they all differ in size. The state House of Representatives is always larger than the state Senate.

Members of the state Senate and House are elected by the voters in each state. The states are divided into voting districts. A voting district is an area where a certain number of people live and vote for their government leaders. There are smaller districts for the House and larger districts for the Senate. In most states the senators serve a four-year term, and the representatives serve for two years.

State Legislators Meet Once a Year

Most state legislatures meet once a year for sixty to ninety days. These meetings of the state lawmaking body are called sessions. If there is an emergency or a special need, the governor or the *legislators* themselves may call a special session.

When the legislature's regular session begins, the members form committees. Each of these small groups has a special task or job to do. These committees handle matters such as education, highways, courts, and local government needs. Bills, which are ideas or suggestions for new laws, are first discussed in committees. These bills are sometimes rewritten or completely rejected by a committee. When bills are ready they

are presented to the entire legislature for approval.

Each house of the state legislature has a presiding leader or official. He appoints committees and their leaders. He conducts meetings or sessions in his part of the legislature. In most states the lieutenant governor is the leader for the Senate. In the

The state legislature, along with the governor, meets in the state's capital city to discuss and vote on bills. This is the state capital building in Annapolis, Maryland.

Organization of One State Government

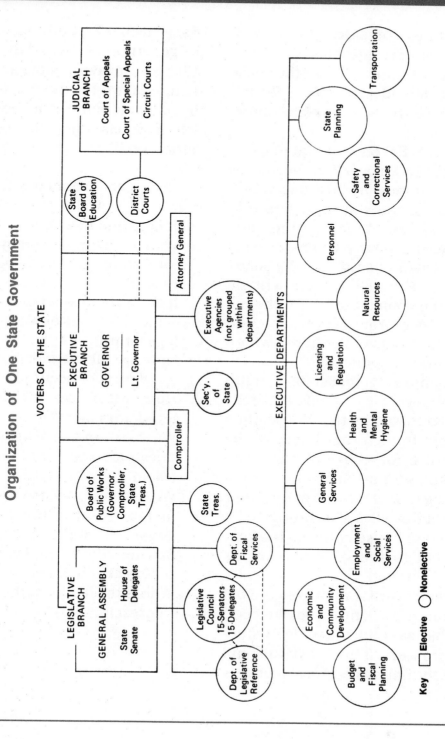

VOTERS OF THE STATE

LEGISLATIVE BRANCH

GENERAL ASSEMBLY

State Senate

House of Delegates

Legislative Council 15-Senators 15-Delegates

Dept. of Legislative Reference

Dept. of Fiscal Services

State Treas.

Board of Public Works (Governor, Comptroller, State Treas.)

Comptroller

EXECUTIVE BRANCH

GOVERNOR

Lt. Governor

Sec'y. of State

Attorney General

Executive Agencies (not grouped within departments)

State Board of Education

JUDICIAL BRANCH

Court of Appeals

Court of Special Appeals

Circuit Courts

District Courts

EXECUTIVE DEPARTMENTS

Budget and Fiscal Planning

Economic and Community Development

Employment and Social Services

General Services

Health and Mental Hygiene

Licensing and Regulation

Natural Resources

Personnel

Safety and Correctional Services

State Planning

Transportation

Key ☐ Elective ◯ Nonelective

other states a president *pro tempore* (temporary president) is elected by the members. In every state the House of Representatives elects its leader, who is called the Speaker of the House.

How a Bill Becomes a State Law

In order for a bill to become a law, it first must be introduced by a member of the state legislature in either house. A committee then receives the bill and begins working on it. Amendments may be made and parts of the bill may be rewritten. When the committee thinks the bill is in proper form, it is presented to all the members of the house where it was first introduced.

For approval most states require a majority vote in favor of a bill. If the bill is approved by that house, then it is sent to the other house of the legislature for consideration. The same steps for making amendments or changes are followed in the other house. If the bill is also approved by the second house of the legislature, it is sent to the governor for his approval or veto.

If the governor approves the bill it becomes law. If he vetoes (rejects) it, the bill may return to the legislature for more work. If the legislature still thinks the bill is a good one members

of the lawmaking body can override the governor's veto and the bill will still become law. In most states this requires a two-thirds vote in favor of the bill. This is the same power that Congress has when the president vetoes a bill.

★Activity E: Number your paper from 1 to 9. Write the answer for each question below.

1. What is the most common name for a state lawmaking body?
2. How many houses make up the legislature in most of the states?
3. Which state has only a one-house legislature?
4. How are all the members of the legislature chosen?
5. How often do most of the legislators meet?
6. What is the name of a small group of legislators who work on a special issue?
7. What are ideas for new laws called?
8. In most states the lieutenant governor is the leader of the Senate. Who is the leader in the other state senates?
9. Who is the leader in the House of Representatives?

PART 6 ★★★ The Executive Branch

WORDS TO KNOW

Mansion
Pardon
Rehabilitation
Superintendent

The executive branch of state government is made up of departments and agencies, and is headed by a governor. Other government officials assist with operating the state. As the chief executive, or leader, the governor has considerable power. His duties are much like the duties of the President of the United States. The governor can appoint heads of departments. He is in charge of drawing up the state budget. The governor is commander in chief of the National Guard. He may "call up" the Guard in time of emergencies such as floods, hurricanes, or riots.

As the chief executive, the governor also has power in the legislative and judicial areas of state government. He may suggest certain bills to the legislature at any time. However, the governor usually does this when he meets with the legislature at the start of each session.

The governor has the power to appoint certain judges who serve in state courts. He may also shorten prison sentences, release prisoners, or even *pardon* a prisoner if special circumstances exist.

How a Governor Is Elected

A statewide election is held to select a governor. The state constitution lists the qualifications for a person seeking the office, including the minimum age. Forty-seven states elect a governor for a four-year term. Only New Hampshire, Rhode Island, and Vermont limit their governors' terms to two years.

Powers and Duties of a Governor

Because of their importance and power, many state governors have later become presidential candidates. Governors who have later been elected president include William McKinley, Theodore Roosevelt, Woodrow Wilson, Calvin Coolidge, Franklin Roosevelt, Jimmy Carter, Ronald Reagan, and William Clinton. Duties include:

- Chief executive of the state.
- Nominates people to fill important state jobs.
- Recommends how money is to be raised and spent.
- Commander in chief of military forces in the state.
- Sends state police and National Guard into areas where they are needed.
- Pardons prisoners in certain cases.
- Proposes laws to the legislature.
- Leader of his or her political party in the state.
- Presides at important ceremonies.

In most states the governor is provided with a place to live. This is often called the "executive *mansion*." Part of the state's chief executive's living expenses may also be paid.

Other State Officials

There are a number of other key officials in the state executive branch. In most states they are elected at the same time as the governor. In a few states they may be appointed by the governor. Among some of the more important state officials are the following:

Governor Wilder of Virginia is pictured here at his swearing in ceremony. As chief executive of the state, his duties are much like those of the President of the United States.

1. Lieutenant governor — The second most important official in a state. This person is elected in thirty-four states. He or she serves as the leader of the state senate in twenty-eight of the states.

2. Attorney general — The chief legal officer in the state. He advises the governor on matters dealing with the law.

3. Secretary of state — This official is usually elected. He keeps all official records, publishes laws passed by the state, and oversees much of the state's official business.

4. Comptroller or state auditor — This individual controls the spending of state money. He is also in charge of keeping financial records for the state.

5. State treasurer — He collects taxes due the state and pays bills owed by the state after they have been approved by the state auditor.

6. *Superintendent* of public instruction — top educational official of the state. He works with the

board of education to carry out the laws and requirements for teaching and learning in the state.

State Agencies

Many departments and agencies exist within the executive branch of each state government. States have grown rapidly in population, and therefore departments have grown in size and number. Most states have a department of human resources, which takes care of such things as public assistance and welfare. It also handles health services and vocational *rehabilitation* (finding employment for the mentally and physically handicapped).

Agencies to protect the environment and to control transportation are part of state governments. Every state has a board of education, with a superintendent or commissioner in charge. A labor board takes care of the problems of labor. A banking commission regulates the banks. Certain professionals and workers in the trades must obtain a license to work in a state. The state has special boards to give examinations to these people and to issue the licenses.

★Activity F: Number your paper from 1 to 7. Match the beginning of the sentence in Part 1 with the correct ending in Part 2. Write the complete sentence on your paper.

Part 1, Beginning of Sentence

1. The executive branch of a state government is...
2. The governor may...
3. The governor can suggest bills...
4. A mansion is usually...
5. The lieutenant governor...
6. The attorney general...

Part 2, Ending of Sentence

a. ...appoint heads of most state departments and agencies.
b. ... is leader of the senate in 28 states.
c. ...headed by a governor.
d. ...is the legal adviser to the governor.
e. ... provided for the governor and his family to live in while in office.
f. ... to the state legislature at any time.

PART 7 ★ ★ ★ The Judicial Branch

W O R D S   T O   K N O W

Boundary	Magistrate
Disorderly	Municipal
Domestic	

E ach state constitution gives the state government the power to keep law and order within the *boundaries* of the state. The legislative branch passes the laws, while the executive branch sees that the laws are carried out. The judicial branch explains the laws and has power to punish those who break them.

State Courts

State courts follow the same principles as federal courts. Cases are divided into civil or criminal cases. Civil cases deal with disputes between two or more parties. Criminal cases deal with violations of the state laws.

The organization of courts is almost the same in each state. Lower courts, trial courts, and a higher court, usually called the state supreme court are typical of state court systems.

Lower State Courts

In some small, rural towns there are justices of the peace. This court official tries civil cases involving small sums of money, performs marriages, and settles minor offenses such as *disorderly* conduct. In larger, more populous areas the role of the justice of the peace is taken over by *magistrate* courts or *municipal* courts.

These lower courts are often separated into special courts that handle only one type of case. Some examples of such special courts are as follows:

- Juvenile court: Hears cases of juveniles (youths under eighteen) accused of breaking the law.
- *Domestic* relations court: Handles disputes or disagreements between husbands and wives and other family problems.
- Small claims court: Settles disputes over small sums of money, usually without a lawyer. This allows people to seek justice without spending a great deal of money.
- Municipal court: This court deals with civil suits, minor criminal offenses, and probate. Probate refers to hearings to settle questions about who should receive the property of someone who has died.

General Trial Court

Serious criminal and civil cases are handled in trial courts. Most cases are heard by a judge and jury. The cases may vary from dishonesty to robbery or murder.

Higher State Courts

The highest court in the state is usually called the state supreme court. If an accused person thinks his case was not tried fairly in a lower court, he may appeal to a higher court. When hearing or considering an appeal, the state supreme court does not hold a new trial. Instead the judges study the records and all the evidence. Then they vote as to whether or not the accused person received a fair trial.

★**Activity G:** Number your paper from 1 to 8. Decide where the actions described below would take place. Write the correct type of court next to each number.

Lower Court
General Trial Court
State Supreme Court

1. An accused person appeals his case to this court because he believes that his trial was not fair.
2. A serious criminal case involving murder is heard by a judge and a jury.
3. The judges study the evidence to decide if a case was tried fairly.
4. A justice of the peace performs a marriage.
5. A girl of sixteen has broken the law. A hearing is scheduled.
6. A dispute between two people led to a serious injury of one person. The case is brought to trial.
7. The judge decides how the property of a person who died should be handled.
8. A worker is charged with stealing tools worth sixty dollars. His case is being heard.

C H A P T E R ★ S U M M A R Y

Since 1788 when the Constitution was approved, the country has grown from the original thirteen states to fifty states. Each state operates under its own constitution. All state constitutions are similar to each other in that the power of the states is divided among three separate branches — legislative, executive, and judicial. Each state has rules and regulations to take care of individual needs. In the United States Constitution, some powers are kept for the states (reserved powers) and some are shared with the federal government (shared powers), such as the power to tax citizens.

A great deal of money is needed to run state governments. The state income tax is the greatest source of income for most states. States use the money to run schools, build roads, provide health and welfare programs, and provide other services, such as police protection, recreation, cultural activities, National Guard, and courts of law.

The legislative branch of the state government has a lawmaking body called, in most states, the legislature. It is divided into two houses — the Senate and the House of Representatives. The members are elected by the voters in each state.

The governor is the elected leader of the executive branch. He appoints heads of departments and can suggest bills to the legislature. He can appoint certain judges and has some control over prisoners (granting pardons). The state has other elected officials, such as a treasurer, a clerk, and an attorney general. Departments and agencies are run by the state to take care of services and the business of the state.

The judicial branch, with its system of courts, applies the laws and punishes criminals. There are three types of state courts: lower courts to handle lesser civil and criminal cases; general trial courts with a judge and jury for more serious cases; and state supreme courts to handle appeals from the other courts.

C H A P T E R ★ R E V I E W

Comprehension:
Identification

Directions: Number your paper from 1 to 10. Next to each number write the word that is missing. Use answers from the words listed below.

income	*welfare*
schools	*constitution*
branches	*governor*
appeals	*attorney general*
serious	*legislature*

Each state in the United States operates under its own 1)___. The power of the states is divided among three 2)___ of government. These state governments need a great deal of money to run properly. The state 3)___ tax brings in the greatest amount of money. States use most of their money to run the 4)___. They also provide health and 5)___ programs.

Most state lawmaking bodies are called the 6)___. The head of the executive branch of a state is called the 7)___. Another elected official of the state who takes care of legal matters is the 8)___. A state also has a judicial branch with a system of courts. The trial courts handle 9)___ cases, both civil and criminal. In most states the state supreme court handles 10)___ from the other courts.

Comprehension:
Understanding Main Ideas

Directions: Write the answers to the following questions using complete sentences.

1. Many state constitutions are very long — much longer than the United States Constitution. Give two reasons why this is true.
2. What are three powers that the states reserved for themselves when writing the United States Constitution?
3. How do state governments spend money to protect the lives and property of its citizens?
4. Who is the chief executive of a state government and name three of his/her duties.
5. What is the job of a state supreme court in appeals cases?

Critical Thinking:
Writing Your Opinion

1. States use several ways to obtain money to run their governments. Can you think of additional ways that states may obtain money?
2. Do you think all of the state officials are necessary? Give reasons for your answer.

CHAPTER TEN

Local Government

 County Government

Local governments were the United States' first governments. When the colonists settled in America they quickly elected leaders and made laws to keep peace and order. Today local government is still the most basic level of government. It protects lives, homes, and provides citizens with safe environments, schools, libraries, and other important services.

State governments decide what type of local government will exist in the state. Some local governments, such as school districts, take care of a single service. Others, such as counties and cities, have several responsibilities. The activities of one or more local governments affect people's lives every day.

Local governments receive charters, or plans of government, from state legislatures. These charters give local governments certain powers, such as the right to tax their citizens, to keep law and order, to own property, to sue and be sued, and to have the same rights as individuals in courts.

County Governments

In forty-six of the states, the local governments are county governments. Connecticut and Rhode Island are divided into counties, but these divisions are not used for local government. Louisiana calls its local units "parishes," while Alaska uses the term "buroughs."

During the early history of the United States, counties existed to take care of the rural areas. For some people in remote sections the county government was the only government they had.

The number of counties varies from state to state. In each county, a city or town serves as the county seat. Like a state capital, the county seat is where county officials have their offices. These offices are often in a county courthouse or county-owned building.

Who Runs the County?

The county government is usually run by a county board, which is a group of elected officials. Some states use other names for this board, such as board of commissioners, board of supervisors, or commissioners court. This board may pass laws regulating public health and welfare matters. The county board may also set the amount of taxes and may oversee road construction within its area. This group of ruling officials usually also makes *zoning* decisions. Zoning regulations are rules about how and where homes and businesses may be built. The county board also supervises the use of all county buildings such as libraries, jails, and court buildings.

Other County Officials

The people who live in the county elect other officials to carry out special duties. The following are officials found in most counties:

1. Sheriff — The chief county law enforcement officer. He carries out orders made by the court. He can arrest people who break the law. Most sheriffs are in charge of the county jail.
2. County Clerk — Keeps records of births, deaths, and marriages in the county. He or she also keeps copies of deeds, which are records of the sale of land or buildings.
3. County Treasurer — Supervises the taking in and spending of money by the county.
4. County Auditor — Examines the county's records concerning money and sees that they are kept properly and legally.
5. Prosecuting Attorney or District Attorney — Represents the county in court cases. He *prosecutes* people who have violated county or state laws.

Some larger counties have more officials, including a purchasing agent, public defender, park commissioner, public health nurse, and a coroner. A coroner is a person who investigates deaths that are violent and deaths that are not attended by a physician.

★**Activity A:** Number your paper from 1 to 8. Choose a word to complete each sentence below. Write the word next to the number.

seat	local
districts	road
county	charters
jail	money

1. Today ___ governments are our most basic level of government. They protect our lives and provide services.
2. Some local governments, such as school ___, take care of a special service.
3. Local governments receive ___ from state legislatures.
4. In forty-six states the local government is the ___ government.
5. Each county has a county ___ where the officials have their offices.
6. The county board manages ___ construction and zoning regulations.
7. The sheriff carries out court orders and is in charge of the county ___.
8. All the taking in and spending of ___ is handled by the treasurer.

PART 2 ★ ★ ★ City Government

WORDS TO KNOW

Cultural   *Urban*
Maintenance

City governments have become more important as the United States has developed. The population of the country has shifted from rural to *urban* areas. City governments manage large numbers of city residents. Some areas of a city may be very crowded. Then it is more difficult for a city government to maintain the safety, health, and education of those citizens.

Some of the everyday responsibilities of a city government are providing police and fire protection; keeping streets repaired; providing clean water; providing public transportation; and providing trash collection.

A city government also provides *cultural* and recreational activities that are an important part of city life. Libraries, museums, parks, gardens, art galleries, and theaters may be supported with city funds.

City Governments Get Charters From the State

State legislatures issue city charters to communities that want to become cities. A charter is a plan of government that outlines the powers given to a city. This charter permits a city to have a governing group separate from the areas around it.

Cities are usually governed by one of three forms of government. The mayor-council is the most common type of city government. The two other most widely used forms of government are the commission and the council-manager type.

Mayor-Council

The chief executive or leader of this type of government is the mayor. Both the mayor and the council are elected by the voters. Each member of the council represents a small area or section of the city, called a ward. Either the mayor or the council appoints the heads of the departments, which operate the city.

Commission

Usually this form of government has no elected mayor. The city is run by a group of commissioners. Sometimes one of them will be selected by the others to act as mayor. He will be in charge of meetings and will represent the commission at official ceremonies.

The voters often elect one commissioner to head each of the city's departments. That person supervises his department's activities and services, which may include garbage collection, police and fire protection, health care, or recreation. These commissioners then work together as a group to manage the city's government.

City Governments Must Provide Police Protection

Of all the services provided by city governments, police protection is probably the most important and most expensive. As cities grow in size and population, it has been shown that the crime rate also grows. This means that police departments in most cities must expand and improve to meet these new demands.

City police departments, with money from the federal government, are teaching policemen the latest crime-fighting and prevention methods. Courts have complained, in the past, that too many criminals were set free because of lack of evidence. Policemen are now being taught how to investigate crimes, question witnesses, and gather evidence. It has been proved that when policemen completely investigate crimes before turning the cases over to detectives, more criminals are brought to justice. This makes cities safer and can reduce the cost of police protection.

Council-Manager

This form, also called the city manager plan, has an elected council that acts as the city's lawmaking body. Under this system, the city is run very much like a business.

The council hires a city manager who handles the city's business under the direction of the council. The city manager appoints department heads who are directly responsible to him. The city manager does not belong to any political party and does not have to run for office. Many people think that this allows the city manager to do the best job possible without having to please the voters.

Other Types of Local Governments

Other forms of local government exist. Small communities may be called towns, townships, villages, or boroughs. Many of these towns and villages have received a charter from the state to operate. Because these communities are much smaller than cities, their government is much simpler. They have fewer departments because not as many services need to be provided. Many of the mayors and council members are not paid. The mayor-council form is most often used in these communities.

New England Towns

Although the New England states are divided into counties, the towns are the basic unit of government. The town has a form of government called direct democracy. This means that all qualified voters meet together to conduct the town's business. Such meetings are held once a year or even more often, if necessary. The town's officers, called selectmen, are elected at the yearly meeting.

This New England type of government dates from colonial times. In those days the meetings were popular events, and almost everyone attended. Today these gatherings are poorly attended, even though the towns have grown. Some towns now elect representatives to attend rather than count on large numbers of the population to be present.

Townships

About sixteen states in the Middle Atlantic and Midwestern regions of our country have townships that provide government for some people. In general, townships are found in the rural parts of counties. People of the township usually elect officials to serve on a board of commissioners or trustees. This board makes rules and regulations for the township. The board may include a tax collector, a clerk, and a justice of the peace.

Villages and Boroughs

Some states allow communities of 200 to 300 families to become villages or boroughs. They are in charge of running their own government. They are allowed to collect taxes, provide for street *maintenance*, set up a fire company, and provide for other services, as needed. Most officials of a village or borough serve on a part-time basis because there is not enough business for a full-time position. When villages become too large, they may ask the state legislature to grant them a city charter.

★**Activity B:** Number your paper from 1 to 10. Choose a word to complete each sentence. Write the correct word next to each number.

state	commissioners
often	rural
departments	boroughs
democracy	more
mayor	mayor-council

1. City governments have become ___ important as our country grows.
2. There are ___ overcrowded areas in some cities.
3. A city government has ___ that are responsible for providing services to the people of that city.
4. A city charter is issued by the ___ legislature.
5. The most common form of city government is the ___ type.
6. If a city has a ___, he may be elected by the voters.
7. In a commission form of government the city is run by a group of ___.
8. New England towns use a direct ___ form of government where all qualified voters meet to elect their leaders.
9. Villages and ___ may operate their own governments.
10. Townships are usually found in ___ parts of some counties.

WHERE DO LOCAL GOVERNMENTS GET THEIR INCOMES?

HIGHLIGHT STORY

★ ★ ★

Counties, cities, and other types of local government need money to provide services for their citizens. Three kinds of taxes are the chief sources of income for local governments: income taxes, sales taxes, and property taxes. Most local governments receive the largest income from property and sales taxes; only some local governments tax incomes.

Sales tax is an easy way of raising money. A tax is placed on special items people buy often. However, in some areas, foods and medicines are not taxed. Some people think that sales tax is not fair because everyone, including the rich and the poor, pay the same amount of tax.

Property taxes provide the largest income for local governments. Property includes the land and the buildings on it. The value of the property is determined by the town, city, or county assessor. The value of the property is then called the assessed value. This is not necessarily the selling price. The assessed value can change as the condition of the property or buildings improve or deteriorate. The local government sets the tax rate on the property, usually a certain dollar amount for every 100 dollars of assessed value. If a town, country, or city needs more money, it can raise the tax rate.

Local governments get their money from other sources. Sometimes bonds are sold to raise money for building projects. A very large amount of money is raised in fees for licenses, such as automobile licenses. Another source of income may come from the federal and state governments. Sometimes as much as one-third of local income is received from the federal and state governments. Many poorer local governments could not operate without this additional financial aid.

Review

Directions: Answer the following questions in complete sentences on your own paper.

1. What are the three major sources of income for local governments?
2. What is property? Who determines what property is worth?
3. What is the value of the property called? What can cause this value to change?
4. Why do some local governments receive financial aid from the federal government and state government?

C H A P T E R ★ S U M M A R Y

Local governments protect the homes, lives, and environment of the citizens who live there. They provide schools, libraries, and other services. County governments, with their elected county boards, take care of rural areas.

City governments are growing in importance as the population shifts from the rural to urban areas. City governments have special problems because of overcrowding and growth. Cities may be run by any one of three types of government — mayor-council, commission, or council-manager.

Towns and township governments are found in some parts of the country. They also provide services to the communities they serve. Small growing areas such as villages and boroughs may decide to set up their own government.

School districts are found in every state. A superintendent or commissioner is in charge of the school district.

C H A P T E R ★ R E V I E W

Comprehension:
Completion
Directions: Number your paper from 1 to 5. Write the correct words to complete the paragraph.

homes	*County*
boroughs	*urban*
City	

Local governments are considered to be the nearest governments. They protect 1)___, lives, and property. 2)___ governments take care of rural areas. 3)___ governments are growing in importance because the population is shifting from the rural to 4)___ areas. Small growing areas, such as villages and 5)___, may also set up their own government.

Comprehension:
Understanding Main Ideas
Directions: Write the answers to the following questions using complete sentences.

1. What are two of the duties of a county board, the group of people who run a county?
2. Why have city governments become more important over the years?
3. What is the most common type of city government? Who is the chief executive of this type of government?
4. What are three other types of local government, besides the county and city?
5. What is a charter and what does it allow a city to do?

Critical Thinking:
Writing Your Opinion
1. According to the text, cities provide many services for their citizens. Can you think of some other ways that cities could use their incomes for the good of its citizens?

CHAPTER ELEVEN

Politics and Voting

 Political Parties

Political parties are made up of groups of people who share common ideas or ways of thinking about government. These groups try to get their candidates into public offices where they will promote or use the group's ideas. Since the late 1770s, political parties have named most of the candidates for Congress, the vice presidency, and the presidency.

Why People Join Political Parties

People have always tended to seek the company of others who have similar interests, beliefs, and needs. People go to places of worship that best express their religious beliefs. They join clubs and organizations that support the interests they value. People form groups to gain more power to protect their property or ideas. It is for this reason that political parties developed.

Throughout history people have had different ideas about how to govern well. They have talked about and used various methods to achieve democracy and individual freedom. Therefore, it was logical that groups representing different approaches to government would appear. Political parties are not mentioned in the Constitution. They exist by custom, not by law.

How Political Parties Developed

Early forms of political parties existed in the country during the colonial times. One group, the Whigs, was opposed to the king and the Parliament, the governing body of England. The other group, the Tories, was loyal to the government of

England. These Tories became known as Loyalists after the colonies broke with England. This is because they remained loyal to the king and to England.

The Federalists and the Anti-Federalists

After the colonists won the Revolutionary War, two groups formed that had different political and economic beliefs. The Federalist Party was made up mainly of *coastal* planters and merchants. This party supported a more powerful central government.

Opposing the Federalists were the Anti-Federalists, who believed that a less powerful central government with strong, independent states would make a better nation. In 1787 the Federalists were responsible for calling the Constitutional Convention, which took place in Philadelphia. At this meeting the Constitution was written.

The Constitution was ratified by the convention and then sent to the states for their approval. Many of the states whose interests were supported by the Anti-Federalists feared that the Constitution gave the central government too much power. They would not ratify it until the Federalists promised to add a Bill of Rights once the new government was established.

The *accomplishments* of George Washington, the first president of the new government, were supported by the Federalists. Although Washington would have liked a government without political parties, he was the first president to put a Federalist (Alexander Hamilton) and an Anti-Federalist (Thomas Jefferson) in his first Cabinet. Having two parties sharing responsibilities was unsuccessful. Later on Washington carried out his duties with the help of only the Federalists.

The Democratic Party Begins

The Federalist Party controlled the government until 1801. It helped create solid beginnings for the new country's government. In 1801 Thomas Jefferson was elected president. Jefferson led the Anti-Federalists, who changed their name to the Democratic-Republican Party. Later this party would be known simply as the Democratic Party. This party was in power most of the time between 1801 and 1861. For short times the Whigs were in power. The Whigs were the successors of the Federalists.

First Sixteen Presidents of the United States

		Party	Began Term
1.	George Washington	None	1789
2.	John Adams	Federalist	1797
3.	Thomas Jefferson	Democratic-Republican	1801
4.	James Madison	Democratic-Republican	1809
5.	James Monroe	Democratic-Republican	1817
6.	John Quincy Adams	Democratic-Republican	1825
7.	Andrew Jackson	Democratic	1829
8.	Martin Van Buren	Democratic	1837
9.	Wm. Henry Harrison	Whig	1841
10.	John Tyler	Whig	1841
11.	James Knox Polk	Democratic	1845
12.	Zachary Taylor	Whig	1849
13.	Millard Fillmore	Whig	1850
14.	Franklin Pierce	Democratic	1853
15.	James Buchanan	Democratic	1857
16.	Abraham Lincoln	Republican	1861

The Issue of Slavery Influenced Political Parties

The question of slavery threatened the unity of the political parties. Both the Democratic and Whig parties were divided, with some members of each group favoring slavery while others opposed it. It was this issue of slavery that led to a final split of the Whigs.

Those persons against slavery organized a new political body, the Republican Party. In 1860, after almost sixty years of mostly Democratic power, the Republicans supported a man who was to become one of America's most famous leaders. That man was Abraham Lincoln.

★**Activity A:** Number your paper from 1 to 8. Match each term in Column 1 with its description in Column 2. Write the correct letter next to each number.

Column 1, Term

1. Political party
2. Constitution
3. Whigs
4. Tories
5. Federalists
6. Anti-Federalists
7. Bill of Rights
8. Republicans

Column 2, Description

a. Favored a strong central government.
b. Later known as Loyalists.
c. A group of people with the same ideas about government.
d. Opposed the Parliament and the king.
e. Supported Abraham Lincoln for president.
f. Makes no provision for political parties.
g. Added to the Constitution.
h. Believed in strong, independent states.

Two Major Political Parties

W O R D S   T O   K N O W
Dedicated   *Progressive*

Although the Constitution did not mention parties, there are two major political parties in the United States. Each party offers candidates for offices, from the presidency to local government.

Many countries in Western democracy have a two-party system. The United States is one. Great Britain is another. A multi-party system makes it possible for the government to represent the majority of the people. This system is also fair to the political party out of power. Usually one of these parties promotes central government control. The other party, however, is usually more *progressive* and believes in less government control. The two major parties that have held most of the power in the United States are the Democratic and the Republican parties.

The Democratic Party

The real beginning of the Democratic Party was in 1827 when Andrew Jackson left the party that Thomas Jefferson started. Jackson felt that the party was being used for the good of the wealthy. He was *dedicated* to the idea that the federal government should represent the common man. Jackson became president in 1828.

The Republican Party

The Republican Party is the other powerful political party in America. It had its beginnings in 1854. It began as a combination of several groups that were against many of the beliefs of the Democratic Party. It was formed primarily in opposition to slavery. Abraham Lincoln, long known for his firm stand against slavery, was nominated by this new Republican Party. In 1860 Lincoln was elected President of the United States.

Political Parties in Power Since 1861

	1861	1865	1869	1873	1877	1881	1885	1889	1893	1897	1901	1905
Democratic							■		■			
Republican	■	■	■	■	■	■		■		■	■	

	1905	1909	1913	1917	1921	1925	1929	1933	1937	1941	1945	1949
Democratic			■	■				■	■	■	■	
Republican	■	■			■	■	■					

	1949	1953	1957	1961	1965	1969	1973	1977	1981	1985	1989
Democratic	■			■	■			■			
Republican		■	■			■	■		■	■	■

Key: ■ In power

The party in power is the party whose candidate is elected President.

ANDREW JACKSON AND THE DEMOCRATIC PARTY

"Let the people rule."

Andrew Jackson, the son of poor immigrants, became an orphan at 14. He later studied law and became a lawyer. He also became an Indian fighter, and was a general in the War of 1812. Because of his successful victory at the Battle of New Orleans, Jackson became a national hero.

Jackson's popularity as a war hero helped him defeat John Adams for the presidency in 1828. He became the seventh president of the United States. He was admired by the farmers and the working men, especially those in the new states in the west. He was one of the founders of the Democratic Party. He fought with Congress and the Supreme Court for the rights of the common people. He demanded a ten-hour working day for laborers. He encouraged the formation of labor unions. He called for banks to be inspected and set down strict rules for the running of banks to protect people's money.

Jackson was president for eight years, but his influence was felt for twenty. This period was called the "Age of Jackson."

Review

Directions: Answer the questions on your own paper using complete sentences.

1. Why did Andrew Jackson become a national hero?
2. Who did Jackson defeat to become president?
3. Which groups of people admired President Jackson?
4. As one of the founders of the Democratic Party, what were some things he believed in?
5. Although he was president for only eight years, why do you think his influence was felt for the next twenty years?

★**Activity B:** Number your paper from 1 to 6. Complete each sentence below with a word from the box.

two-party   slavery
Democratic   Jackson
Lincoln

1. The United States is one of a number of countries that have a ___ ___ political system.
2. ___ was dedicated to the idea that government should represent the common person.
3. The two parties that have held most control in the United States are the ___ Party and the Republican Party.
4. The Republican Party was formed in opposition to ___.
5. ___ represented the Republican Party in the election of 1860.

PART 3 ★ ★ ★ Minor Parties

W O R D S   T O   K N O W
Campaign   Prohibition

Even though the United States is a country with a two-party system, there are also some less powerful political parties. These minor parties are referred to as third parties. They do not have the strength of the Democratic Party or the Republican Party, but they have had an important place in American political history.

From time to time people who want to run for office find that their political beliefs are different from those of the Democrats and Republicans. Therefore, to be considered for office, they have to be nominated by a third party. Even though these candidates have little chance of being elected, they do have an influence on the election outcome. It is possible for them to attract votes from one of the major candidates, thereby swinging the election in favor of the other party. This happened in 1912 when a third party, the Progressive Party, ran Theodore Roosevelt for president. Roosevelt did not win but he drew votes away from William Taft, the Republican candidate. Because of this, the election was won by Woodrow Wilson, the Democratic nominee.

Third Party Ideas Have Influence

Some of the ideas of third parties may become part of the beliefs of the major parties who may not have agreed with them at first. Third parties have dealt with issues such as the abolition (ending) of slavery, states' rights, *prohibition,* women's suffrage (right to vote), and the abolition of child labor.

Minor Parties Have Limited Success

Minor parties have many obstacles standing in the way of their success. They usually do not have the financial support they need to promote their candidates and programs. Newspapers, television, and radio usually do not give minor party candidates much attention. In most cases a minor party stands for only one issue. It may depend on the name of one person who is known for some popular issue, such as states' rights or religious concerns.

In 1968 Governor George Wallace of Alabama formed the American Independent Party and was its candidate for president of the United States. Even though he was not elected, Wallace won a large number of votes. His *campaign* had a major effect on the outcome of the presidential election. Many Democrats voted for Wallace, thus allowing Republican candidate Richard Nixon to be elected with less than fifty percent of the nation's popular vote.

★Activity C: Number your paper from 1 to 5. Complete each sentence in Part 1 with the correct ending in Part 2. Write the correct letter next to each number.

Part 1, Beginning of Sentence

1. Minor parties are referred to as…
2. In 1912 the Progressive Party…
3. Third parties have dealt with issues like…
4. Some obstacles standing in the way of third parties are…
5. In 1968 Governor George Wallace of Alabama…

Part 2, Ending of Sentence

a. …states' rights, prohibition, women's suffrage, and abolition of child labor.
b. …the lack of financial support and little attention from the newspapers and television.
c. …third parties.
d. …formed the American Independent Party.
e. …ran Theodore Roosevelt for president.

PART 4 ★ ★ ★ The Parties in Action

Political parties exist for many reasons. They have certain policies that they believe in. They try to present candidates who will uphold these beliefs. Of the two major parties, the Republicans *traditionally* have been politically *conservative*. The Democrats have been more *liberal*. However, within the parties are groups with special interests that differ in some ways from the party's main stand. An example of this is the Southern Democrats, who have always been more conservative than the Democrats in other parts of the United States.

Every four years party members come together for a convention. This is where they nominate candidates for president and vice president. They prepare statements about what these candidates plan to do if elected. These statements of policy and promises are known as a *platform*.

A platform committee is made up of delegates from each state and territory of the country. They listen to suggestions and ideas for the platform even before the convention begins. They put these ideas together, and during the convention they present a report on the platform. Sometimes the platform is accepted as presented. Sometimes certain parts of it are debated and even changed before the entire convention will accept the platform. The high point of the convention, of course, is when the candidates for president and vice president are nominated.

Other Functions of Political Parties

Besides nominating candidates and writing party platforms, political parties also have a number of other functions. They keep the public informed about what is going on in government at all levels (federal, state, local). They point out issues they feel are helpful or harmful to the people so that the public can understand how they are affected. When a party's candidate is in office, the party helps govern by seeking support for the official as he or she tries to put party policy into action. When a party is not in power, it is called the opposition party. Members of the opposition party watch the party in power very closely. They point out changes in government they would like to see made, and suggest how this might be done. They always hope this will help their party in future elections.

★Activity D: Number your paper from 1 to 10. Complete each sentence below. Write the correct word next to each number.

state	*territory*
differing	*platform*
issues	*four*
power	*presidential*
conservative	*ideas*
parties	

1. Republicans traditionally have been more ___ than Democrats.
2. Sometimes members of the same party have ___ beliefs about good government.
3. National party conventions take place every ___ years.
4. A ___ is made up of statements of beliefs, policies, and candidates' promises.
5. The high point of a convention comes when the ___ candidate is nominated.
6. The platform committee is made up of delegates from each ___ and ___ of the country.
7. Political parties often point out ___ they think are helpful or harmful to people.
8. The opposition party closely watches the actions of the party in ___.
9. Political ___ have certain policies that they believe in.
10. The platform committee listens to ___ for the platform before the convention begins.

PART 5 ★ ★ ★ State Primary Elections

W O R D S   T O   K N O W

Ballot   Indirect

The word primary means "first in order." Therefore, the term primary election means the election that is held first, before the general election.

Political parties use the primary election method to choose members of their party to run for public office in a general election. A narrowing-down process takes place in the primary. Any number of possible candidates might run for a nomination in a primary. However, only one candidate from each party is chosen to run for an office in a general election. Then, in the general election, voters select the winning candidate.

Direct Primary

There are several types of primaries. The form most often used is the direct primary. In this type party members who wish to run for office may request that their names be put on the *ballot*. Then they are voted on directly by the voters. There are two kinds of direct primaries: open and closed. An open primary has ballots for all the candidates. Voters may choose both the party

and the candidate of their choice when they are in the privacy of the voting booth. A closed primary requires voters to declare in advance which party they want to vote for. They can vote only for candidates of that party.

Indirect Primary

In an *indirect* primary delegates to party conventions are selected by members of that party rather than by the voters. Then at the party convention, these delegates choose candidates who will represent that party in the election.

Nonpartisan Primary

Nonpartisan primaries are connected to no special political party. This type of primary is generally used for smaller local elections. Only a candidate's qualifications are considered by the people who vote.

Presidential Primary

One other type of primary is the presidential primary. Some states use this method to select delegates for the national convention. These delegates have promised to support a certain candidate. The candidate presents his or her delegates at the convention. A vote for those delegates is the same as a vote for the candidate who presented them. A similar method is the presidential preference primary. In this primary voters choose delegates in the same way, but the delegates do not have to support certain candidates.

★Activity E: Number your paper from 1 to 4. Write the kind of primary that each statement refers to.

Direct, open primary
Direct, closed primary
Indirect primary
Nonpartisan primary

1. The voters choose the party and the candidate.
2. Only delegates to a party convention are chosen.
3. No political party is involved. This type of primary is used for small, local elections.
4. A voter declares which party he or she is voting for and then votes for the candidates of that party.

PART 6 ★ ★ ★ National Political Conventions

W O R D S   T O   K N O W
Keynote   *Unity*

Every four years political parties hold national conventions to select their candidates for president and vice president, and to develop a party platform. These conventions take place before the November presidential elections. Citizens have the opportunity to follow the proceedings of the convention by television, radio, and printed news media.

Each major party has a national committee which selects the site for the convention. It also tells each state and territory how many delegate votes it will have. Sometimes a state or territory chooses to send more delegates than it has votes. When this happens some delegates can cast only part of a vote.

Convention delegates are chosen in different ways: some in primary elections, some by state or district conventions, and some in presidential primaries. A delegate and an alternate are selected for each vote that a state or territory has. If for any reason the delegate is unable to vote, the alternate votes.

Before the national convention, candidates campaign across the country to win support of delegates. At the convention these candidates work to win unpledged delegate votes until the moment votes are cast. The successful candidate becomes the party's nominee for the national election.

The Keynote Address

After the national committee chairman calls the convention to order, the *keynote* address is given. This speech is made by an important party member who usually praises the national party, asks for cooperation among its members, and predicts party victory in the coming national election.

Committees Run the Convention

Four committees organize and run each national convention. Each state and territory is allowed one member on each committee. These committees are:

1. Organization — Nominates the permanent chairman and other officers of the convention.

2. Rules — Sets the rules and procedures for running the convention.

3. Credentials — Settles any dispute about which delegates from a state or territory may vote.

4. Platform — Develops and writes the principles and policies for the party. In writing the platform, the committee members usually try to include the ideas and views of the person who is most likely to be named the party's presidential candidate.

In 1988, Vice President George Bush campaigned to become the next president. He attended many rallies to gather voter support.

The Convention Proceeds

When the committees have completed their tasks and the party platform is approved by the delegates, the convention begins nominating people to be the party's presidential candidate.

Many speeches are given explaining why each person should be the nominee. The supporters of each major candidate often stage noisy demonstrations of enthusiasm. These demonstrations are meant to make other delegates think about voting for that candidate. After the first roll call, when every state and territory has been asked in alphabetical order if it wants to nominate anyone, the nominating is complete. Although most states do not offer a candidate, some states present the names of "favorite sons" — individuals who usually do not have a chance of being elected but who are highly respected by that state's delegates.

Once again, the party chairman calls the roll. He asks each state and territory whom that state wants to support with its votes. Sometimes a candidate will win the party's nomination on the first roll call. This is often the case when a popular president has been nominated for a second term. However, when there are several popular candidates, the roll calls can go on for several days. Often a favorite son candidate will ask his supporters to change their votes to another candidate. This can help that person to be nominated.

Once the presidential candidate is named, he quickly meets with his advisers and decides on his choice for the vice presidential nomination. Traditionally the party nominates the individual the presidential candidate suggests.

The convention ends with the acceptance speeches of the newly named candidates. After the convention these candidates and their supporters face several months of campaigning. Presidential candidates usually try to bring together all the candidates who opposed each other during the primary campaigns. This shows *unity* to the nation's voters and improves the party's chances of winning the November election.

★**Activity F:** Number your paper from 1 to 6. Write the answer for each question.

1. What is the main duty of a delegate to a political convention?
2. What does the credentials committee do?
3. What is one way supporters show that they favor a candidate?
4. What does the term "favorite son" mean?
5. Why is it sometimes necessary to have several roll calls when voting at a convention?
6. Who chooses a party's candidate for vice president?

PART 7
★ ★ ★
Political Campaigns

W O R D S   T O   K N O W
Donations   *Fund-raising*

A political campaign is made up of those things that are done in an effort to get a candidate elected to a political office. A political campaign is the busiest between the time a candidate is nominated by his or her party and the time of the general election. However, some people who hope to be nominated may campaign for many months, or even years to win the party nomination and then the election. They use a great deal of energy convincing their party and the voters that they are best for a certain position.

A political campaign can be simple or complicated, depending on the importance of the office. The amount of competition for the office also affects the type of campaign. A person running for governor, state congressman, senator, or mayor of a large city must have a well-organized campaign. These campaigns will also require a large amount of money. The most expensive and best organized campaigns are those carried on by candidates for national offices such as the presidency.

A big national campaign takes a great deal of money and many volunteers who work without being paid. Candidates are limited as to how much money they may accept as *donations* and how much they may spend on their campaigns. This is to make it difficult for any group to "buy," or unfairly influence a candidate to take care of their interests.

Raising Money to Run a Political Campaign

Many committees are involved in political campaigns, and a *fund-raising* committee is one of the most important. This group may seek money by appealing to supporters by mail. They may plan functions like dinners or barbecues, and sell tickets to people who wish to attend. Special interest groups who feel the candidate will support their ideas help out financially. A candidate's own political party contributes some of the money to the campaign. Most candidates put up much of their own money. Because of the great expense, it is difficult for many people to run for public office.

Why Money Is Needed

Money is needed for many different activities in a campaign. A campaign for a national election needs offices and staffs all over the country. The expense of paying the staffs and running the offices is large. That is why candidates depend so heavily on volunteers who donate their time to the candidate. Advertising on radio and television, in newspapers and on posters, costs a great deal of money. Mailing letters requesting the support of voters is another expense. Candidates who travel from place to place to meet voters have to pay for the cost of travel. Often

As a representative of the people, a candidate for political office must campaign to gain support from the voters.

candidates have planes, trains, or buses that take them and their workers all over the country. This expense is one of the biggest of a campaign.

A Campaign Staff

A campaign staff is usually made up of men and women who have worked with the candidate for a long while. They may even be personal friends.

Organization of a Typical Campaign Staff

Campaign Manager — Plans and runs the campaign.

Press Secretary — Handles contacts with news media.

Fund Raiser — Seeks money contributions.

Treasurer — Pays the bills of the campaign.

Advertising Director — Sees that the candidate becomes well known.

Poll Taker — Conducts polls to see how popular the candidate is.

★**Activity G:** Number your paper from 1 to 10. Answer these questions about the chart above.

1. What are two things needed to run a big national campaign?
2. What are three ways money may be raised to run a political campaign?
3. What are some expenses of a national campaign?
4. Who makes sure that a candidate becomes well known?
5. Who decides on the plan for running the campaign?
6. Who pays the bills of the campaign?
7. Who handles contacts with the press?
8. For whom does the campaign staff work?
9. Who looks for ways to raise money?
10. Who conducts polls to find out how popular the candidate is?

PART 8 ★ ★ ★ The Right to Vote

Barrier   *Dishonorable*

The right to vote is given and protected by the Constitution. This freedom to have a voice in choosing leaders is considered to be a privilege by many United States citizens. Unfortunately, all citizens do not take advantage of their right to vote. They may lack interest. They may feel that their vote would not make any difference. They may not know how to register to vote. Some nonvoters may feel that their government is running well and no change is needed. Other nonvoters may not have the qualifications to vote.

The qualifications to be a voter are few and simple. No one may be denied the right to vote because of race, color, sex, or religion. These rights are called "civil rights." Some people were kept from voting by threats of violence or loss of job if they went to the polls until the Civil Rights Acts of the 1950s, 1960s, and 1970s were passed. These civil rights laws did away with these *barriers* that interfered with citizens' freedom to vote.

After a long struggle, the Nineteenth Amendment was ratified in 1920, giving all American women the right to vote.

Who May Register to Vote

In all the states except North Dakota, a voter must register in his or her own county. At age 18 a United States citizen must be allowed to vote if he or she has all the other qualifications. A person must have lived in a state for a certain period of time. Although the length of time varies from state to state, it is generally thirty days. Most states will not let a person vote if he or she is mentally ill and committed to a hospital. Persons who have been convicted of certain serious crimes may not be permitted to vote. Some states will not permit anyone to vote who has received a *dishonorable* discharge from the armed forces.

Federal, state, and local government employees may vote, but must follow certain rules when taking part in political activities. The Hatch Acts, passed by Congress in 1939 and 1940, say that a government worker may not hold public office, serve as a delegate to a political convention, or serve as a candidate's campaign manager.

Registration

Qualified persons who wish to become voters must register in the voting district of their residence. A person may register at the courthouse of the voting district. Sometimes other places of registration will be set up. The names of persons who register will be recorded on the district's list of qualified voters. These lists of voters are important. Otherwise people could vote more than once in different places and cause elections to be dishonest. Another reason for registration is to have a record of which voters live in certain places and who may legally vote on local matters.

Any voter who votes regularly is considered an active voter. If a voter fails to vote in a certain number of elections, his or her name will be taken off the list of active voters. To vote again the person would have to reregister. Some states require voters to reregister from time to time, even if they do vote. Officials feel that they can keep more accurate

---

Susan B. Anthony: A Fighter for Women's Rights

American women have had to fight for their right to vote. A few states gave women this privilege in the 1800s. However, it was not until 1920 that the Nineteenth Amendment to the Constitution was ratified. This amendment gave women throughout the country the right to vote.

Susan B. Anthony (1820-1906) was a heroine of the women's suffrage movement. She worked hard to help women win the right to vote. At one time she was the publisher of *Revolution* magazine, which published articles about rights. Once she was even arrested for voting! Her trial called attention to the cause for which she was working. During her lifetime she saw a number of states allow women to vote, but she died fourteen years before all American women were given the right to vote by the Nineteenth Amendment. She is remembered for her contribution to the welfare of women.

---

records of active voters this way. They can then drop from their lists the names of inactive voters who fail to register.

Casting a Ballot

Special places, called polls, are set up where people can vote. Often schools or church halls are used for this purpose. Officials working at the polls check their records for a voter's name before they allow him or her to vote.

Voting may be done by a paper ballot or by a machine that shows the ballot. A ballot is a list of all candidates, the parties they represent, and sometimes suggested bills or amendments. The ballot usually organizes the information in one of two ways. About half of the states group the names of candidates according to the office they are seeking. This means that the names of candidates of all parties are all mixed together under the title of the office. The other states group candidates first by party and then by office.

Today, voting is done in the privacy of a voting booth. Privacy is an important part of the election process. Early in the country's history, people were required to vote by voice or by raising their hands.

Later, when ballots were first used, different sizes and colors were made for each candidate, so others were able to see whom a person voted for. Today when paper ballots are used, care is given to use the same size and color. This helps the voting process to be honest.

Voting Districts

Boundaries of voting districts are set according to the number of people living within them. As populations change, these boundaries may have to be redrawn. In the United States, the population has been moving from rural areas to the city, so urban areas need more representatives and rural areas need fewer representatives. This redistricting has not always been done fairly. Certain court cases during the past few decades have pointed to this problem. Great effort has been made by honest officials to organize the districts so that each citizen will be fairly represented in both federal and state governments.

Absentee Ballots

If a citizen is not going to be in his own voting district for a primary or general election, he may request an absentee ballot, in person or by mail. This is a ballot available for a certain length of time before the actual election day. The ballot may be marked and turned in ahead of time.

★**Activity H:** Number your paper from 1 to 7. Complete the sentences below with words from the list. Write the correct word next to each number.

privacy	record
population	polls
ballot	absentee
qualifications	

1. Some people cannot vote because they do not have the ___.
2. One reason for registration is to have a ___ of people who may legally vote.
3. Special places set up for people to vote are called ___.
4. A ___ contains the names of all candidates to be voted on.
5. Today voting is done in the ___ of a voting booth.
6. Redistricting is necessary when ___ changes occur.
7. An ___ ballot is used by people who are not going to be in their own voting district at election time.

PART 9 ★ ★ ★ How People Can Help Make Laws

W O R D S   T O   K N O W
Controversy   Mandatory

In addition to voting for candidates for public office, voters may also vote on how they feel about certain issues. Their votes can bring about new laws.

The Referendum

Certain bills are presented to voters at the polls for them to accept or reject. This process is called a referendum. This takes place only at the state level. There are different kinds of referendums.

Petition Referendum

After a law is passed by the state legislature, citizens may circulate a petition for signatures objecting to the law. If enough people show their objection by signing this document, the petition referendum will be placed on the ballot. Voters may then cast a vote for, or against, the law at the polls. Enough opposing votes will kill the law.

Optional Referendum

In some states the legislature may choose to refer a proposed law to the public for acceptance or rejection.

This is called an optional referendum. In this case, the legislature is not forced by law to refer the law to the voters, but it does so willingly. Usually the issues referred to the public are those which have caused a great deal of *controversy*.

Mandatory Referendum

When state laws require that certain issues be sent to the voters for their approval or rejection, a *mandatory* referendum is used. For example, a state may use a mandatory referendum to change its state constitution. Delaware is the only state that may change its constitution without public approval.

Initiative

In some states citizens can suggest a new law to be presented to voters. This suggested law is called an initiative, or a proposition. A petition must be signed by a certain number of people before the initiative can be voted on by the legislators or by the citizens. If a majority are in favor of the law, it goes into effect.

Recall

If citizens believe that an elected official needs to be removed from office before his or her term has expired, they may use the recall process. They must draw up a petition, get a great number of signatures, and meet certain legal requirements. Then the recall issue is placed on the ballot. If a majority of the voters are in favor of the recall, the elected person must leave office.

★**Activity I:** Number your paper from 1 to 5. Write Yes or No for each question below.

1. Are referendums used at the state level?
2. Do voters ever have a chance to approve or reject suggested laws?
3. May states change their constitutions?
4. Can one person ask for an initiative to be placed on a ballot?
5. Can an elected official be voted out of office?

C H A P T E R ★ S U M M A R Y

Political parties are groups of citizens who share many of the same beliefs about government. These groups support candidates who agree with their ideas. Political parties have existed since colonial times. The original political groups — the Whigs, Tories, Federalists, and Anti-Federalists — developed into two present-day parties. These are the Democratic Party, led in the early period of the country's history by Thomas Jefferson and Andrew Jackson, and the Republican Party, which grew out of an anti-slavery movement and the presidency of Abraham Lincoln.

Minor, or third, parties appear from time to time. Although no third party candidate has ever been elected president, minor party nominees do affect election outcomes. They take votes from major parties, and they call attention to certain issues.

Most states hold primary elections where voters choose both candidates for the general election and delegates to political conventions. The delegates usually support a certain candidate. These conventions are followed by the general election, where the voters actually choose the office holder.

Every four years national conventions are held where delegates decide on candidates and party policies for the coming election. The conventions are followed by political campaigns. The candidates spend several months trying to convince voters that they should be elected to office. These campaigns are expensive and require a great deal of money to pay for staff advertising, and travel. Volunteers are necessary so that campaign costs may be kept as low as possible. Laws regulate where campaign money can come from and how much a candidate may accept.

The Constitution guarantees citizens the right to vote. Still, many groups, such as women and minorities, have had to struggle for this right. Citizens consider voting a privilege, but some do not vote.

States decide who may vote by requiring certain qualifications. However, the federal government sees that voting requirements and practices are fair for all groups.

A person must register before he or she can vote. Each voter's name must be recorded on a list of qualified voters a certain number of days before the election. This record helps keep track of properly-qualified voters and reduces dishonesty in voting.

Most voting today is done on a voting machine, although some areas use handmarked ballots. All voting is done in the privacy of a voting booth.

Voting districts are set up according to population so that each citizen's vote will count the same as any other person's. As population changes take place, redistricting is necessary.

In addition to voting for candidates, people may also vote on ideas for new laws or changes in existing laws. The processes of presenting the laws directly to the voters are called the referendum and the initiative. Voters may also use the recall process to remove an elected official from office should it become necessary to do so.

C H A P T E R ★ R E V I E W

Comprehension:
Recalling the Facts
Directions: Number your paper from 1 to 10. Write the answer to each question below.

1. What are the two major political parties?
2. Why are third parties important?
3. Which election takes place first — the primary election or the general election?
4. How often are national political conventions held?
5. What is the purpose of a national political convention?
6. Why are political campaigns expensive?
7. Do all voters have to register first?
8. Do voters in all the states have to meet the same requirements?
9. Why do Americans value their right to vote?
10. Citizens can vote for the candidate of their choice. What else might be on a ballot for a voter to consider?

Comprehension:
Understanding Main Ideas
Directions: Write the answers to the following questions using complete sentences.

1. What issue led to the creation of the Republican Party? What famous American was supported by the Republican Party in 1860?
2. What is the purpose of a state primary election?
3. How is the vice presidential candidate chosen?
4. All citizens over the age of eighteen may vote in elections if they are registered. Which groups of people are not allowed the privilege of registering to vote?
5. What is a ballot? What are two ways that voting may be done?

Critical Thinking:
Writing Your Opinion

1. National political campaigns take a great deal of money and each year it increases. How do you think the cost of running a national campaign may be limited or decreased?
2. Although citizens are strongly encouraged to vote many do not. What do you think can be done to encourage more people to vote?

CHAPTER
TWELVE

A Look at Other Governments

PART 1 **Governments Are Different**

W O R D S   T O   K N O W
Adopt   *Principle*

In this chapter you will learn about different forms of government and how they operate. Many governments, including the United States, are democracies. Comparisons will be made between the democratic government of Great Britain and the United States.

You will learn about countries that are not democracies. One of these countries was the Union of Soviet Socialist Republics (U.S.S.R.). This country was commonly called the Soviet Union. Its government was run by the Communist Party. You will discover some differences between democracy and communism. You will also learn how the lives of citizens are involved with the governments in these different systems.

The United States Government is a Democracy

Governments, in some form, have existed for as long as people have lived together in groups. The government of the United States of America developed over the years into the form we know today. It is a constitutional government. The government is run by rules and laws written into the Constitution.

The authors of the Constitution had learned from the past. They *adopted* the best ideas from other systems of government. The Constitution calls for a group of states to be joined together by the laws of a national central government. The United States government is a democracy because it is based on the *principle* that people are important. It is run by the people and serves the people.

Many other countries have similar democracies based on a constitution.

These are known as constitutional democracies. They are also based on the principle that the people are the most important part of the nation. Rules and laws in these democracies are made to benefit individuals and to protect their rights and freedoms.

On the other hand, there are systems of government in the world based on the principle that the country itself is more important than the people who make up the country. They believe that people have a strong responsibility to serve the country. This is the basis of Communist governments in some nations. Most decisions are made by the government. The people have little say in running the government or in making the laws that control their lives.

★Activity A: Answer these questions using complete sentences. Write the answers on your own paper.

1. What type of government does the United States have?
2. Why are rules and laws in a democracy based on a constitution?
3. What are the basis or beliefs of a Communist government?
4. Who makes decisions in a Communist government?
5. What part do individual people play in making laws in a Communist government?

PART 2 ★★★ Democratic Forms of Government

W O R D S   T O   K N O W
Parliamentary

Many countries have democratic governments. The people of these countries depend on their elected representatives to make the laws and rules that keep their freedoms safe. Two important forms of democracy are those that have *parliamentary* leadership and those that have presidential leadership.

Parliamentary Leadership

Many forms of government give all of the power to one central group of people. Often this group of elected officials is called a parliament. The government of Great Britain is a good example of this. Although the British government is really a constitutional monarchy, the Parliament holds the power. It makes the laws and elects the prime minister, who is the chief executive. The Parliament holds all of the legislative power and all of the executive power. Local governments exist, but only

to help Parliament with some of its duties. This type of government is democratic because the people elect the leaders that represent them. Many other countries have parliamentary leadership, including Japan, Israel, and Spain.

Presidential Leadership

A government with presidential leadership divides the power between a central group and several local groups. Sometimes this division is described in a constitution, as in the United States. The constitution

Comparing Government Systems

	United States	Great Britain
FORM OF GOVERNMENT	Presidential leadership Federal system, with three branches of government Two-party system	Parliamentary leadership One government body, the Parliament Multiple parties
LEADER	President elected by the people	Prime Minister elected by Parliament
PERSONAL FREEDOM	Guaranteed by the Constitution	Guaranteed by common law and carefully observed tradition.

describes how the power of government is to be divided.

In the United States, certain powers are held by the national, or central, government. Other powers are given to the states, or local governments. The chief executive, or president, is head of the executive branch. He is elected by popular vote. The legislative power is given to another branch. The state governments also have executive and legislative branches. Some countries that follow this form of presidential leadership are the United States, Mexico, and Switzerland.

★Activity B: Number your paper from 1 to 6. Each sentence beginning in Part 1 has its ending in Part 2. Choose the letter of the correct ending. Write that letter next to each number.

Part 1, Beginning of Sentence

1. In a democracy...
2. In democratic countries with parliamentary leadership...
3. In democratic countries with presidential leadership...
4. All of the power in the British government...
5. In the United States and other countries with presidential leadership, local governments...
6. In countries with presidential leadership, the chief executive...

Part 2, Ending of Sentence

a. ...the executive and legislative power is held by one central group.
b. ...is elected by popular vote.
c. ...the central, or national, group separates the legislative and executive powers.
d. ...the people depend on elected representatives.
e. ...is held by the Parliament.
f. ...also have the power to make laws and elect officials.

THE GOVERNMENT AND THE OPPOSITION

As in the United States, there are two major political parties in Great Britain. These are the Conservative Party and the Labour Party. During a general election members of the House of Commons are chosen. When the election is over, one of these two parties will have more seats than the other. This party is the majority party and is known as the "Government." The other party is known as the "Opposition." This term comes from the word oppose, which means "to be against something." One party is opposed to the other.

Both the Government and the Opposition have important roles. The leader of the Government is the prime minister. The prime minister chooses the Cabinet and department heads from members of the Government party. The policies and ideas of the Government are put into practice when this winning party takes over.

The Opposition party keeps check on the party in power by questioning. Four days a week a question period is held in the House of Commons for this purpose. The Opposition uses this time to present their views. The Opposition is always trying to win the support of the members and return to power.

Review

Directions: On your own paper, answer these questions with one word answers.

1. One of the two major political parties in Great Britain is the Conservative Party. What is the other?
2. What is the majority party in the House of Commons called?
3. Who is the leader of the "Government"?
4. Which party keeps check on the party that is in power?
5. What does the prime minister choose from members of the Government party?

PART 3 ★ ★ ★ Comparing Two Governments

W O R D S   T O   K N O W
Ceremony   *Generation*
Figurehead

Two islands form the nation of Great Britain. The larger island includes England, Scotland, and Wales. The northern part of the second island is called Northern Ireland. The southern portion of this island is the independent country of Ireland, which is not part of Great Britain. The people who live within Great Britain are called English, Irish, Scottish, or Welsh, depending on where they live. Often people from these countries are simply called British.

Great Britain's parliamentary form of government is quite different than the United States' presidential form. Although the forms may be different, both countries are democracies and have been for a long time. The United States has had its form for more than two hundred years, while Great Britain has had its present form of rule for almost three hundred years. Both governments are based on a constitution, but they are quite different.

The United States Constitution is a carefully worded document. The language used has allowed for great flexibility in interpretation over many years. Only part of Great Britain's constitution is in writing. This is made up from the laws passed by Parliament, from old documents such as the Magna Carta, and from common law. Common law is a group of laws based on customs of the people. The unwritten part of the British constitution includes many traditions, especially the way the Cabinet and the monarch work together.

The chief executive of Great Britain is the prime minister. The prime minister is elected by the controlling party in Parliament, and is formally appointed by the monarch. He or she is not elected as directly by the people as the President of the United States is.

A second difference between the parliamentary and presidential forms of government is that the British Parliament has one strong, central branch of government which makes the laws and sees that they are enforced. The United States government has three branches to balance and separate the power.

A third difference between the two systems is the use of the veto, the power to reject or refuse new legislation. While the president has the power to veto a bill and uses it from time to time, the prime minister does not have such a power. Although the monarch of Great Britain does have veto authority, it has not been used since the early 1700s.

A Monarchy That Is Run Like a Democracy

Great Britain is officially a monarchy because the head of the government is a king or queen. This title and position is inherited, which means that it is handed down from *generation* to generation. Great Britain has been ruled by Queen Elizabeth since 1952. The queen is a *figurehead*, a symbol of the British government. She approves laws passed by Parliament, although they can become laws without her approval. She signs all important documents and makes speeches to Parliament from time to time. The people look forward to her appearances at *ceremonies* and special events. The queen and members of the royal family are highly respected and honored by the British citizens. However, the country's government is run by the prime minister

and elected officials, making it a democracy.

The British Parliament Has Two Houses

The government of Great Britain is run by a lawmaking body called the Parliament. Parliament works much like the United States Congress. Parliament is made up of two houses, the House of Lords and the House of Commons. Only the members of the

Queen Elizabeth remains a highly honored symbol of monarchy to British citizens, even though the British government is actually a democracy.

House of Commons are elected. A member of the House of Lords receives his or her membership by inheriting it or as an honor granted by the government. Unlike the United States Congress, where both houses are elected, Parliament has only one elected house.

The House of Lords

The House of Lords has about one thousand members. This group examines all bills proposed by the House of Commons. Although the House of Lords cannot reject a bill, they can delay its passage. The House of Commons can make a bill a law by voting to approve it two years in a row. The House of Lords also serves as the highest court in Great Britain. It hears cases on appeal from the lower courts, just as the United States Supreme Court does.

The House of Commons

The real power of Parliament is held by the House of Commons. Its 650 members make the laws. One of its members from the majority party becomes prime minister. The prime minister, in turn, selects the heads of government departments. The members of the House of Commons come mainly from the two major political parties in Great Britain, the Conservative Party and the Labour Party. The Conservative Party usually prefers a gradual change; the Labour Party is usually supported by the workers.

★Activity C: Number your paper from 1 to 7. To which country does each sentence refer? Write *United States* or *Great Britain* by each number.

1. This country's government is run by a strong legislative branch called Parliament.
2. Scotland is part of this country.
3. This country's government has three separate branches.
4. This legislative branch of the country's government is called Congress.
5. The House of Lords and The House of Commons are part of this country's legislature.
6. The highest court in this country is the Supreme Court.
7. All members of this country's legislature are elected.

PART 4 ★ ★ ★ Some Governments Are Not Democracies

One type of government that is not a democracy is a dicta–torship. In a dictatorship, all power is held by one person or a small group of people. The people have little say in how the government is run. Two important examples of dictatorships in the twentieth century are Fascist Italy (1922–1943), and Nazi Germany (1933–1945). The rulers in both of these nations killed individuals who opposed them.

Another form of government that is not democratic is *communism*. Russia, later renamed the Soviet Union, was the first Communist coun–try. The Soviet Union tried to help other countries around the world to establish Communist governments. After World War II, Communist gov–ernments took power in several coun–tries that bordered the Soviet Union. Also, the People's Republic of China, the Socialist Republic of Vietnam, and the Republic of Cuba established Communist governments.

In the mid 1980s, a new leader–ship in the Soviet Union began to question the nation's system of government. The Soviet Union's economy was in serious trouble. The Communist system of government had failed to provide the people with enough food and other consumer goods. For the first time in history, a Communist government tried to make major changes in its system of government. These changes led to a collapse of the government. In order to understand what happened to the Soviet Union, it is necessary to under–stand how the Communist system worked.

Communist Government of the Soviet Union (1917–1990)

The Communist government of the Soviet Union came into power in 1917. The king at that time, called the czar, was overthrown; and the Communists took over. Under this new rule, the government ran all the industries such as iron, steel, oil, coal, and railroads. The large homes and property of wealthy people were divided up among the peasants, or poor people, of the country. Also small farms joined together to form larger farms, called collective farms. Factory workers and farmers were urged to give up personal comforts to strengthen the country's indus–try. The Soviet people lived under many government restrictions. The government controlled many indus–

tries and most of what was printed in newspapers.

Private ownership of businesses and property had increased in the late 1980s, but was still restricted. This was very different from the United States, where private ownership is encouraged.

How the Soviet Government Was Organized

The Soviet Union was made up of fifteen republics. A lawmaking body, called a soviet, was set up for each republic. Actually, these councils had very little power. They could only carry out the laws made by a group called the "Supreme Soviet." The Supreme Soviet was made up of representatives from the fifteen republics. It made the laws for the whole nation. It also ran the departments of the government that handled such things as finance, defense, foreign affairs, industry, and agriculture. The republics made few of their own laws. In the United States, the individual states make many of their own laws, although Congress makes laws for the whole country.

The head of the government was called the "premier." He was the chairman of a group called the "Council of Ministers," who were appointed by the Supreme Soviet. The Council of Ministers had a great deal of power. It had more power than the President of the United States or a prime minister. All of the leaders of The Soviet Union were members of the Communist Party, the only political party in the nation.

The Importance of the Communist Party

In the United States and other democracies, at least two major political parties with different ideas are always trying to gain control of the government. This had not been the case in the Soviet Union where there had only been one political party — the Communist Party. The government accepted all the deci-

Communist Government of the Soviet Union

Premier
- Chief Administrator

Council of Ministers
- About 95 members
- Controlled the economic and cultural life
- Controlled foreign relations.

Supreme Soviet of the U.S.S.R.
- Two-house legislature
- About 1,500 members
- Passed laws proposed by Communist Party leaders
- Appointed members of the Council of Ministers

sions of the party and made them into law. All the members of the government were also members of the Communist Party. In fact, the person who held the position of general secretary of the Communist Party was considered to be the most powerful person in the Soviet Union. The premier and general secretary were often the same person.

In contrast, the United States government is made up of people who belong to different political parties, with different views. Even within one party, members have different ideas about running the government. The final decision about how the government is to be run is made by the voters.

When a Soviet citizen voted, there was only one candidate for an office. If the voter did not favor that candidate, he or she could cross out the name. Sometimes voters were afraid to cross out the name because they did not have complete privacy in voting. Unless one-half of the voters crossed out a name, the candidate was elected. Few candidates ever lost an election. Failure to vote in the Soviet Union was a serious matter and could have been reported to the police.

★**Activity D:** Number your paper from 1 to 6. Complete each sentence in Part 1 by choosing its correct ending in Part 2. Write the correct letter next to each number.

Part 1, Beginning of Sentence
1. The Soviet Union did not run...
2. In the Soviet Union the government controlled...
3. Private ownership of business and property in the United States is...
4. The Supreme Soviet, made up of representatives from the republics,...
5. The head of the government in the Soviet Union...
6. There was only one political party in the Soviet Union and...

Part 2, Ending of Sentence
a. ...not only allowed but is encouraged.
b. ...was called the premier.
c. ...most of the industry.
d. ...made laws for the whole nation.
e. ...its government as Democratic countries do.
f. ...it made the decisions for the government.

PART 5 ★★★ Organization of the Communist Party

WORDS TO KNOW

Assembly   *Quotas*
Politburo

Many small Communist Party groups existed throughout the Soviet Union. One of the duties of members was to act as a "watchdog" for the party. For example, members observed how their fellow factory workers did their jobs. They checked to see if factory managers met their *quotas*. Workers lost their jobs if they did not please the party group where they worked. Most of the important positions in the workplace were filled by Communist Party members. It was difficult for people to get ahead in the Soviet Union if they did not belong to the Communist Party. All these small groups and other larger groups were joined together by the *Politburo*. The powerful members of the Politburo made most of the important decisions for the party.

Political Parties in Democratic Countries

In the United States and other democratic countries, people may join any political party they choose. This could be one of the major parties or a third, or minor, party. They may choose not to join any party at all. This freedom of expression is one feature of democratic forms of government. Because most industry in the United States is privately owned and operated, political parties are not concerned with work quotas. This is the concern of the owner of the business and his desire to make a profit. Workers in most Democratic countries are not hired, promoted, or fired because of the political party they belong to.

The Soviet Constitution

The Soviet Union had a written constitution just as the United States and other countries do. It had been rewritten three times in the last sixty years. Before 1990 one important part of the constitution pointed out that the Communist Party was the guiding force behind the government. This article of the Soviet constitution stated in part:

"The leading and guiding force of Soviet society and the nucleus of its political system…is the Communist Party of the Soviet Union."

In contrast the United States Constitution makes no mention of political parties. The parties were free to develop over the years.

Constitutional Rights, Freedoms, and Duties

The Soviet constitution mentioned "rights, freedoms, and duties," just as the United States Constitution does. Rights, such as freedom of speech, press, and *assembly,* were allowed in the Soviet Union. Their constitution granted these rights but only "with the aims of building communism." There had been many reports in the international press of Soviet citizens being arrested for speaking out against the government. Newspapers usually printed the news after it was approved by a government agency. The Communist Party had an official news agency called Tass, that selected the news to be released to the public.

In the United States there is no government agency telling the newspapers what to print. Newspapers are not owned by the government as they are in the Soviet Union. The owners of the newspapers in the United States decide what to print.

Attempts to Change the Soviet Government

In 1988, a serious attempt to change the Soviet system of government had begun. Many of the changes were designed to make the Soviet government more democratic. The Supreme Soviet approved changes in the constitution that would set up a new legislature of parliament. The new 2,250–member legislature was called the "Congress of People's Deputies." It essentially replaced the 1500–member Supreme Soviet. A secret ballot was used to elect 1500 deputies. The remaining 750 representatives would be chosen by

Even though religion is a great part of Russia's history, only recently have the people been allowed to attend church gatherings.

members of the Communist Party, trade union and other groups.

Unlike the Congress of the United States, the Congress of People's Deputies met at least once a year. The deputies elected a new Supreme Soviet of 542 members. This smaller Supreme Soviet met often. The deputies also picked a president who in turn appointed a premier. The new president had authority over foreign policy, defense, and social and economic affairs. On May 25, 1989,

Not Everyone Could Join the Communist Party

A person who wished to join the Communist Party in the Soviet Union had to apply and go through an investigation before he or she was accepted. Young people between the ages of 14 and 18 had to be members of the Young Communist League. This was a youth group that taught and trained children in party ideas. All people who applied spent a year working for the party to show that they were loyal. After one year of probation passed, a person then became a member of the party. Every workplace in the Soviet Union — factory, government office, school, store, village, collective farm, or armed forces station — had a small Communist Party group of loyal members.

Congress of the People's Deputies met for the first time. The majority of the elected deputies were workers or teachers. Few were professional politicians.

More changes were still to come. In February of 1990, the powerful Central Committee of the Soviet Communist Party agreed to eliminate the section in the constitution that made the Communist Party the "guiding force" behind the government. It was a historic change; other political parties had been banned in the Soviet Union since 1921. However, the Communist Party still played a "leadership role" in Soviet affairs.

The loss of total political control upset some of the Communist party members. In August of 1991, a group of them tried to take over control of the Soviet Union's government. Their attempt failed, and the Soviet Union soon collapsed. Several republics declared their independence. Others continued to try to work together. Even these republics elected their own leaders. The republics of the former Soviet Union are struggling to form new governments and to improve living conditions.

How democratic the republics become remains to be seen. Never before has a Communist nation collapsed. The republics face major challenges. It is uncertain whether the republics will set up more democratic forms of government or return to Communist-controlled rule.

★**Activity E:** Number your paper from 1 to 7. Choose the correct word to complete each sentence from the words given. Write your answer next to each number.

1. The Soviet Union had been made up of (five, fifteen) republics.
2. In (democratic, Communist) countries, people may join any political party they choose.
3. Before 1990 the constitution of the (Soviet Union, United States) stated that the Communist Party was the guiding force behind the government.
4. The United States Constitution makes no mention of political (elections, parties).
5. The Soviet constitution mentioned freedom of speech, but there were press reports of citizens being (arrested, concerned) for speaking against the government.
6. Workers in most (Communist, democratic) countries are not hired because of the political party they belong to.
7. After many decades the (Soviet Union, United States) tried to make changes in its government.

C H A P T E R ★ S U M M A R Y

All countries are ruled by some form of government. Many are democracies. Other countries have systems of government run according to the ideals of the Communist Party.

Democratic countries usually follow the parliamentary or presidential form of government. In the parliamentary form all power to make laws (legislative power) and to carry out the laws (executive power) is given to a single group, often called a parliament. An example of this is the government of Great Britain. In the presidential form the legislative and executive powers are given to separate groups. This type of government is found in the United States.

Great Britain and the United States

Although Great Britain and the United States are both democracies, their governments operate in different ways. The British prime minister is not elected by direct popular vote as our president is. He or she is the leader of the majority party in the House of Commons, one of the two houses of the British Parliament. The other house is the House of Lords. Only members of the House of Commons are elected; the Lords receive their titles by inheriting them, or as an honor. Great Britain also has a monarch who serves as a figurehead.

Both the United States and Great Britain have two major political parties. One party or the other is usually in control of the government in these countries.

Communism and Democracy

In countries run by the Communist Party, such as the former Soviet Union, the government is very powerful. Historically there is only one political party for voters to choose candidates from — the Communist Party. In the United States, Great Britain, and other democratic countries, candidates come from two or more political parties. Citizens may vote for any candidate and join any political party. In the Soviet Union citizens could have joined the Communist Party only if they were accepted. They had to prove themselves by working hard for a year before they could become members. Small groups of these members were found in all places of work.

The Soviet constitution does include rights and freedoms for its citizens, but everything had to be done for the benefit of the Communist Party. Freedom of press and speech were limited. If a person spoke out against the government, he or she could have been arrested. The government also limited what news the public might know. In the United States, citizens may speak out against the government and its leaders.

Recently the Soviet Union collapsed. Some republics declared independence and some are working to try to form new governments and improve the economy.

C H A P T E R ★ R E V I E W

Comprehension:
Completion

Directions: Number your paper from 1 to 10. Choose the correct word or words to complete each sentence. Write your answer next to the number.

1. (Democratic, Communist) countries usually follow either the parliamentary or presidential form of government.
2. An example of a country with the parliamentary form of government is (Great Britain, the United States, the Soviet Union).
3. An example of a country with a presidential form of government is (Great Britain, the United States, the Soviet Union).
4. The (president, prime minister) is not elected directly by popular vote.
5. The members of the House of (Commons, Lords) receive their titles by inheriting them.
6. The United States and Great Britain each have (one, two, three) major political parties.
7. In countries run by the (Political, Communist) Party, the government controls almost everything.
8. Loyal Communist Party members act as (leaders, watchdogs, members) for the party in all places of work.
9. In the United States citizens (may, may not) speak out against the government.
10. In (democratic, Communist) countries citizens are allowed to take part in private groups.

Comprehension:
Understanding Main Ideas

Directions: Write the answers to the following questions using complete sentences.

1. What group of elected officials holds all the power in Great Britain? Name two powers that this group has.
2. Name one difference between the parliamentary and presidential forms of government.
3. What is the oldest form of government that is not democratic?
4. According to the constitution of the former Soviet Union, what was the guiding force behind the government?
5. What is one difference between how people received news reports in Communist countries from people living in democratic countries?

Critical Thinking:
Writing Your Opinion

1. Why do you think Great Britain still has a monarch, even though this person is only a figurehead?
2. What form of government do you think the republics of the former Soviet Union will choose?

CHAPTER
THIRTEEN

Citizenship

 PART 1 **United States Citizens**

W O R D S   T O   K N O W

Famine   *Refuge*
Immigrant   *Refugee*
Naturalization   *Revolution*
Persecution

The United States is sometimes called a "melting pot." This is because people of many different races and nationalities live there. An American citizen may have a great-grandfather who was German and a great-grandmother who was Irish. These nationalities become mixed when the great-grandparents married while living in the United States. The citizen is not German or Irish, but American. Even though a great deal of "melting" has taken place in America, many people keep some of the culture, traditions, and customs of their family members who first settled in this country.

A person may be an American citizen by birth. A person who was born in another country may become an America citizen through a process called *naturalization*. All American citizens enjoy many rights. Citizens have many responsiblities including respecting the rights of others.

Why People Came to the United States

The first settlers came to the United States to gain the freedom they did not have in the countries of their birth. Through the years *immigrants* have come to the United States in great numbers. Many were escaping unfair treatment or seeking the freedoms guaranteed by the United States Constitution.

Certain groups immigrated to the United States at different times for different reasons. For example, *revolutions* and *famines* drove people from their own lands. These people chose the United States as the land of *refuge* and opportunity. Large numbers of immigrants came as laborers.

Limits on Immigration

One period of time when few immigrants came to this country was during the Great Depression in the 1930s. There were so few jobs available then that many Americans were out of work.

Between 1900 and 1930 most immigrants to the United States came from Europe. A law was passed in 1965 placing limits on the number of people who were allowed to immigrate to the United States. As the law is now, there is a set number of immigrants who may be admitted to the United States each year. The number of immigrants from any one country has a limit. In certain situations, *refugees* from political or religious *persecution* are also allowed. Examples of this are the Vietnamese and Cambodians who came to the United States after the Vietnam War.

Often more people wish to come to the United States than the yearly limit allows.

Then each case is judged by itself. People who have relatives in the United States have a better chance of being admitted than those who do not. People who have special talents or job skills may qualify over those who do not.

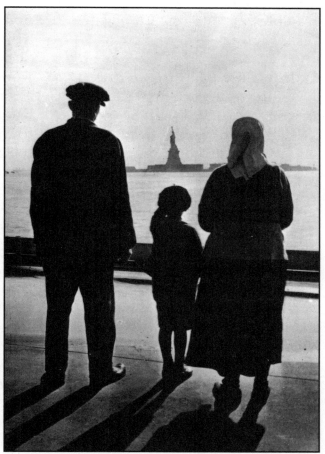

During the immigration wave of the early 1900s, many Europeans arrived at New York Harbor. The Statue of Liberty was a symbol of refuge and freedom for the immigrants.

IMMIGRANTS CONTRIBUTE TO THE UNITED STATES

Immigrants and their offspring have enriched the American way of life. Two examples are Andrew Carnegie and Cesar Chavez.

Andrew Carnegie

Andrew Carnegie and his family arrived in America from Scotland in 1848. He was twelve years old. His family was quite poor. Every member tried to work hard and to be honest. Andrew had a number of low-paying jobs during his youth. His hard work helped him advance in the companies where he worked. Carnegie finally went into the steel business. He made a fortune by the time he reached middle age. Carnegie believed in sharing his wealth. He gave millions of dollars to education, libraries, and the cause of peace.

Cesar Chavez

Cesar Chavez was born in Arizona in 1927. His parents were of Mexican birth and had come to the United States from Mexico. When Cesar was a boy, he and his family became migrant farmworkers in California. Migrant farmworkers harvest crops, and move from place to place as the crops ripen and need to be picked. Chavez dedicated his life to helping farmworkers. He organized the poor and underpaid workers. By using peaceful means, he helped them get better pay and working conditions. Change did not always come easily. Under Chavez's leadership the grape pickers refused to work for almost five years. Finally the farm owners agreed to give the pickers work contracts and higher pay.

Review

Directions: On your own paper, answer these questions using complete sentences.

1. What business helped Andrew Carnegie make his fortune?
2. How did Carnegie share his wealth?
3. What type of work did Caesar Chavez and his family do?
4. What group of workers refused to work for almost five years? What was the result of this work stoppage?

★Activity A: Number your paper from 1 to 6. Complete each sentence in Part 1 with its ending in Part 2. Write the correct letter next to each number.

Part 1, Beginning of Sentence

1. The United States is sometimes called a "melting pot" because...
2. A person born in the United States...
3. Immigrants may become naturalized citizens by...
4. Many immigrants have come to the United States to...
5. During the Great Depression of the 1930s...
6. After the war in Vietnam, many Vietnamese and Cambodians...

Part 2, Ending of Sentence

a. ...doing certain things required by law.
b. ...escape mistreatment, famines, and revolutions in the countries of their birth.
c. ...people of many different races and nationalities live here.
d. ...becomes a United States citizen at birth.
e. ...came to this country as political refugees.
f. ...there were few jobs available in the United States.

PART 2 ★★★ Types of Citizenship

W O R D S   T O   K N O W

Deport
Diplomat
Native
Naturalization

Most Americans are native-born. This means they are citizens simply because they were born in the United States or in one of its territories. A person born to American parents in a foreign country is also a United States citizen. In most cases, a child born to foreign parents in the United States is considered to be a United States citizen. The parents of these children must be living in the United States at the time of the child's birth. This is not true for people representing other governments in this country, such as *diplomats*. They are subject to the laws of their own country; therefore their children become citizens of their parents' *native* country. When there is any question about whether or not a person is legally a United States citizen, the matter must be settled by the Department of Justice.

Naturalization

Aliens are persons who are citizens of another country but who are in the United States for a particular reason. While they are in the United

States, they must abide by the laws of the country. They enjoy most of the rights of American citizens. These people may be visitors or they may have temporary jobs in the United States and plan to return to their own countries. However, many aliens hope to become citizens of the United States. It is possible for them to do so by means of a legal process called *naturalization*. For whatever reasons they are in the United States, aliens must register once a year in January with the United States Immigration and Naturalization Service.

The Immigration and Naturalization Service, an agency which is part of the Department of Justice, is in charge of laws having to do with aliens. The agency says who may enter this country, who may be naturalized, and who is to be *deported*. An alien who is deported must leave the United States and return to the country of his or her birth. There are many reasons why an alien might be deported. The person may have committed a serious crime. Perhaps the person is loyal to some government that is unfriendly to the United States.

Rules for Naturalization

Congress has made rules for aliens to follow in order to become naturalized citizens. These rules say that aliens must:

1. Be at least eighteen years of age.
2. Have lived in the United States for
   a. five years, or
   b. three years if married to a United States citizen, or
   c. less time if the person has served a year in some branch of the armed services.
3. Make an application, or a request, for naturalization to the immigration authorities.
4. Be able to speak, read, and write English reasonably well.
5. Have two witnesses testify that they are good, honest people.
6. Know about the history of the United States and its government.
7. Take an examination about United States history and government.
8. Promise not to support any government or belief that would overthrow the government of the United States.
9. Make an oath of loyalty to the United States in court before a judge.

After aliens have successfully done these things, they become citizens of the United States, with all the rights and privileges of citizens by birth. There is an exception to this rule. No former alien may become president of the United States. The children of naturalized citizens automatically become citizens when their parents do. These children must be under the age of 18 and living in the United States at the time.

It is possible for naturalized citizens to lose their citizenship. This can happen for a number of reasons. Usually it is because the aliens were dishonest and untruthful about themselves when they became naturalized citizens. Taking away citizenship has to be done by court order. The proper process of law must be followed.

Political Asylum

The United States also offers to aliens a protection called political asylum. The word "asylum" refers to a place of safety. Political asylum means a place where a person is safe from the dangerous actions or beliefs of his or her own country or government. They may be visitors, athletes, artists, sailors, or workers for another government who feel mistreated by their own countries. The United States offers protection to such people until it is clear why they wish to leave their native lands.

Statue of Liberty

The Statue of Liberty stands on Liberty Island in New York Harbor. Made of copper hammered on iron, it stands 151 feet tall. A newly restored "Miss Liberty" was given a one hundredth birthday celebration during the Fourth of July week in 1986. This symbol of freedom was a gift to the United States from France and dedicated by President Grover Cleveland in October of 1886. Through the past hundred years, the sight of the statue has greeted great numbers of immigrants as they sailed into New York Harbor.

Near to Liberty Island is Ellis Island. It was an immigrant station until 1954. Many immigrants to the United States were required to stay there for a period of time to determine whether they were eligible to enter the country.

A bronze plaque on the Statue of Liberty seems to give an invitation to all who would seek freedom in the United States. It contains the words from the poem, "The New Colossus," by Emma Lazarus, who befriended immigrants. It reads:

Give me your tired, your poor,
Your huddled masses yearning to breathe free,
The wretched refuse of your teeming shore.
Send these, the homeless, tempest—tossed to me;
I lift my lamp beside the golden door!

If reasons for their actions are strong enough, the aliens are allowed to stay. They may apply for United States citizenship just like other aliens.

★**Activity B:** Number your paper from 1 to 10. Complete each sentence with a word from the list below. Write that word next to the number.

aliens   January
deported   Immigration
citizen   Justice
birth   naturalization
asylum   country

1. Most Americans are citizens by ___.

2. A person born to American parents in a foreign country is a United States ___.

3. Children born in the United States to parents who represent another government become citizens of their parents' ___.

4. Questions about who is legally a United States citizen are settled by the ___ and Naturalization Service.

5. Citizens of other countries who are in the United States are called ___.

6. Aliens must register with the Immigration and Naturalization Service each ___.

7. The Immigration and Naturalization Service is an agency of the ___ Department.

8. An alien who is ___ is forced to leave this country and return to his or her own country.

9. The legal process a person must go through to become a United States citizen is called ___.

10. A person seeking ___ is looking for a safe place to live.

PART 3 ★ ★ ★ Rights of Citizenship

W O R D S   T O   K N O W
Acquitted   *Impartial*

Responsible people realize that they must give as well as take if they want to get along with other people. This is the way that family members, classmates, friends, and governments can get along. No single group or person can have things their way completely. Sometimes, a compromise is necessary.

A compromise was made at the First Congress that met in New York in 1789 after the Constitution was approved. Some Anti-Federalist members of the Congress, including Thomas Jefferson, felt that the Constitution gave too much power to the federal government. They were afraid that American citizens could lose some of the rights they had struggled so hard to get. These men agreed to accept the Constitution only if it contained a Bill of Rights. They thought that the Constitution should clearly state the rights individuals were entitled to. The rights the Anti-Federalists asked for are explained in the next section. After they were approved, the first ten amendments to the Constitution became known as the Bill of Rights.

Rights Requested by the Anti-Federalists

1. Citizens should have freedom of religion, speech, press, assembly (to gather together in groups), and petition (to make requests concerning government and laws).
2. Citizens should have the right to bear arms (have guns for protection).
3. Government should not station troops (soldiers) in people's homes without their permission.
4. No unreasonable searches or seizures of homes or businesses can be made without a warrant.
5. Before a person can be tried, he or she must be indicted (accused after evidence has been studied) by a grand jury. A grand jury investigates the charges against a person accused of a crime and decides if a trial should be held. There must be a good reason for a trial. No one may be tried for the same crime twice. A person who is *acquitted* is free of the charge forever.
6. Persons accused of crimes have the right to a speedy trial before a fair jury that is *impartial*.
7. A jury must be used if more than twenty dollars is involved in a lawsuit.

8. No one can be made to pay extremely high bail or fines and must not be given punishment that is cruel and unusual.

9. Individuals have rights other than those listed in the Bill of Rights. Any right not written is known as a reserved right.

10. If certain powers are not given to the federal government or denied to the states, then these powers belong to the states.

★Activity C: Number your paper from 1 to 11. Write the number of the amendment beside the right that it guarantees.

1. Right to bear arms.
2. Right to a speedy trial before a fair jury.
3. Rights other than those listed in the Bill of Rights.
4. No unreasonable searches or seizures without a warrant.
5. Freedom of religion.
6. No cruel or unusual punishment.
7. Freedom of speech.
8. Freedom of the press.
9. No trial without indictment (a list of charges).
10. Freedom of assembly (to gather in groups).
11. Freedom of petition (requests concerning government laws or regulations).

PART 4 ★ ★ ★ Using the Rights of Citizenship

W O R D S   T O   K N O W
Capable   *Criticisms*

Certain rights are guaranteed to all American citizens. No two human beings are exactly alike. Each person is born with different talents and abilities. No two people look exactly alike or act just the same. In school, everyone does not make the same grades. Not everyone has the same academic or athletic ability or the same artistic or musical talent. In the business world everyone is not *capable* of doing the same job. Some people become rich and famous while others lead simple, quiet lives. So, what does the Declaration of Independence mean when it says, "...All men are created equal..."?

Equality among citizens is based on opportunities and rights. American citizens are born with the rights described in the Constitution and its amendments. Naturalized Americans automatically receive them with their citizenship. Even though these rights do not have to be earned, they do have to be protected. Citizens do this by using their rights wisely and respecting the rights of others.

What are some of the responsibilities citizens have in using and protecting their rights? What is the proper use of a right? What is not a proper use? Some of the rights and responsibilities contained in the first ten amendments are described in the following chart.

How Some Rights May or May Not Be Used	
Right:	Freedom of Religion
Citizens May:	Worship as they please and join any church they wish.
Citizens May Not:	Interfere with anyone else's religious freedom.
Right:	Freedom of Speech
Citizens May:	Speak their feelings, even about government, without fear of punishment.
Citizens May Not:	Harm others with their speech or prevent others from speaking freely.
Right:	Freedom of Assembly
Citizens May:	Gather in groups to discuss issues or to demonstrate peaceably.
Citizens May Not:	Assemble to cause a riot, hurt people, or damage property.
Right:	To Bear Arms
Citizens May:	Own approved firearms for purposes of recreation and protection.
Citizens May Not:	Use firearms in unlawful ways.
Right:	Reserved
Citizens May:	Enjoy certain rights not listed in the Bill of Rights, such as to travel freely anywhere in the country.
Citizens May Not:	Use these reserved rights to do anything unlawful.
Right:	Freedom of the Press
Citizens May:	Publish opinions and *criticisms* of issues without fear of punishment.
Citizens May Not:	Publish false statements or pictures that would harm an individual or group.

Duties of Citizens

Rights and protections could not survive unless citizens took their duties seriously. These include civic duties — support of the government, observance of laws, and defense of the country. Political duties include taking part in government procedures by voting for representatives who will best serve the people.

Even before citizens are old enough to vote, they can still serve their country and communities by studying in school about their government. They can learn about good citizenship by participating in school and community projects that require cooperation and a democratic attitude. In school these projects might include playing in the school band, taking part in student government, and respecting school rules, teachers, and fellow classmates. In the community young citizens can hold membership in clubs that promote patriotism. They can also volunteer time to one of many community groups that help other people achieve a better quality of life.

An important duty for all citizens is to gain a knowledge of laws that affect them and their communities. They are expected to obey the laws. They are encouraged to express their opinions about which laws they feel are serving the people well and which laws they feel are not. Young people can prepare for the day when they will be voters by keeping up with current events in local, state, national, and international communities.

★**Activity D:** Number your paper from 1 to 10. Answer the questions. Write *Yes* or *No* next to each number.

1. May citizens worship as they please?
2. May citizens assemble to start a riot?
3. May citizens say how they feel about the government without fear of punishment?
4. May citizens own approved firearms to use for hunting?
5. May citizens publish lies in order to hurt a certain group?
6. May citizens gather for peaceful demonstrations?
7. May citizens publish their opinions and criticisms of current affairs without fear of punishment?
8. May citizens use their reserved rights to break a law?
9. May citizens use firearms in unlawful ways?
10. May citizens enjoy rights that are not listed in the Bill of Rights?

C H A P T E R ★ S U M M A R Y

The United States is known as a "melting pot" because its citizens represent many nationalities. Throughout the history of the United States immigrants from many lands have flocked to its shores. The first settlers were escaping what they felt was unfair treatment in the countries of their birth. Other settlers came to escape famine and revolutions or to have an opportunity to improve their lives.

Between 1900 and 1930, a large number of immigrants came to the United States from Europe. More recently the largest number of immigrants have come from Asia and Latin America. There are limits on how many immigrants are admitted from different countries. Our country offers a home to refugees. It also grants political asylum to people who defect from their countries for strong reasons.

Anyone born in the United States or in its territories becomes a United States citizen. Anyone born of American parents anywhere in the world also becomes a United States citizen. However, children born to people representing their governments in the United States are not United States citizens. An alien is someone who was born in another country but who is in the United States as a visitor, worker, or student. An alien may become a naturalized United States citizen by meeting certain requirements.

United States citizens are guaranteed special rights by the Bill of Rights. Citizens also have duties. Some of these duties are required by law. Responsible citizens do more than what is required by law. They take an interest in government. They take part in community activities, and they vote regularly. When citizens carry out their duties and respect the rights of others, the quality of life is made better for everyone.

C H A P T E R ★ R E V I E W

Comprehension:
Identification

Directions: Number your paper from 1 to 17. Choose words from the list below to complete the paragraphs. Write the correct word next to each number.

revolution	*Asian*
unfair	*European*
famine	*rights*
asylum	*student*
investigated	*law*
alien	*world*
political	*vote*
duties	*wisely*
government	

The first settlers came to America to escape 1)___ treatment. Later other people came to escape 2)___ or 3)___. Some came to better their lives. Before 1930 most of these immigrants came from 4)___ countries. Now most immigrants come from 5)___ and Latin American countries. America also offers a home to religious or 6)___ refugees.

An 7)___ is someone born in another country and who is in the United States as a visitor, worker, or 8)___. An alien is required to do certain things by 9)___ in order to become a United States citizen. People born in the United States or born of American citizens anywhere in the 10)___ are United States citizens.

A foreigner who feels that he is mistreated may seek a place of safety, or political 11)___, in the United States. This person is 12)___. If his reasons are accepted, he may remain and apply for citizenship.

United States citizens have certain 13)___ given by the Bill of Rights. Citizens also have 14)___ that are required by law. Responsible citizens also learn about their 15)___. They 16)___ regularly. They use their rights 17)___.

Comprehension:
Understanding Main Ideas

Directions: Write the answers to the following questions using complete sentences.

1. If a person is not a citizen of the United States by birth, how else can he or she become a citizen? Name two requirements for a person to become a new citizen.
2. Under what conditions can a person lose his or her United States citizenship?
3. According to the Bill of Rights, what must be done before a person is brought to trial?
4. American citizens are given the right to assemble in groups. How can this right be misused?
5. What are two duties of every good citizen?

Critical Thinking:
Write Your Opinion

1. Do you think the United States government should increase the limits on the number of people who may immigrate to the United States? Why or why not?
2. All citizens have basic individual rights that are guaranteed by the Constitution. Which do you think is the most important right you enjoy as a citizen?

APPENDIX A

★ ★ ★

The Declaration of Independence

Adopted in Congress July 4, 1776
The Unanimous Declaration of the
Thirteen United States of America

The Preamble

When, in the course of human events, it becomes necessary for one people to dissolve the political bands which have connected them with another, and to assume among the powers of the earth, the separate and equal station to which the laws of nature and of nature's God entitle them, a decent respect to the opinions of mankind requires that they should declare the causes which impel them to the separation.

A Declaration of Rights

We hold these truths to be self-evident, that all men are created equal, that they are endowed by their Creator with certain unalienable rights, that among these are life, liberty, and the pursuit of happiness. That to secure these rights, governments are instituted among men, deriving their just powers from the consent of the governed. That whenever any form of govern-ment becomes destructive of these ends, it is the right of the people to alter or to abolish it, and to institute new government, laying its foundation on such principles and organizing its powers in such form, as to them shall seem most likely to effect their safety and happiness. Prudence, indeed, will dictate that governments long established should not be changed for light and transient causes; and accordingly all experience hath shown that mankind are more disposed to suffer, while evils are sufferable, than to right themselves by abolishing the forms to which they are accustomed. But when a long train of abuses and usurpations, pursuing invari-ably the same object evinces a design to reduce them under absolute despotism, it is their right, it is their duty, to throw off such government, and to provide new guards for their future security.

A Bill of Indictment

Such has been the patient sufferance of these colonies; and such is now the necessity which constrains them to alter their former systems of government. The history of the present King of Great Britain is a history of repeated injuries and usurpations, all having in direct object the establishment of an absolute tyranny over these states. To prove this, let facts be submitted to a candid world.

He has refused his assent to laws, the most wholesome and necessary for the public good.

He has forbidden his governors to pass laws of immediate and pressing importance, unless suspended in their operation till his assent should be obtained; and when so suspended, he has utterly neglected to attend to them.

He has refused to pass other laws for the accommodation of large districts of people, unless those people would relinquish the right of representation in the legislature, a right inestimable to them and formidable to tyrants only.

He has called together legislative bodies at places unusual, uncomfortable, and distant from the depository of their public records, for the sole purpose of fatiguing them into compliance with his measures.

He has dissolved representative houses and repeatedly, for opposing with manly firmness his invasions on the rights of the people.

He has refused for a long time, after such dissolutions, to cause others to be elected; whereby the legislative powers, incapable of annihilation, have returned to the people at large for their exercise; the state remaining in the mean time exposed to all the dangers of invasion from without, and convulsions within.

He has endeavored to prevent the population of these states; for that purpose obstructing the laws for naturalization of foreigners, refusing to pass others to encourage their migration hither, and raising the conditions of new appropriations of lands.

He has obstructed the administration of justice, by refusing his assent to laws for establishing judiciary powers.

He has made judges dependent on his will alone, for the tenure of their offices, and the amount and payment of their salaries.

He has erected a multitude of new offices, and sent hither swarms of officers to harass our people, and eat out their substance.

He has kept among us, in times of peace, standing armies without the consent of our legislatures.

He has affected to render the military independent of and superior to the civil power.

He has combined with others to subject us to a jurisdiction foreign to our constitution, and unacknowledged by our laws; giving his assent to their acts of pretended legislation:

For quartering large bodies of armed troops among us;

For protecting them, by a mock trial, from punishment for any murders which they should commit on the inhabitants of these states;

For cutting off our trade with all parts of the world;

For imposing taxes on us without our consent;

For depriving us in many cases, of the benefits of trial by jury;

For transporting us beyond seas to be tried for pretended offenses;

For abolishing the free system of English laws in a neighboring province, establishing therein an arbitrary government, and enlarging its boundaries so as to render it at once an example and fit instrument for introducing the same absolute rule into these colonies;

For taking away our charters, abolishing our most valuable laws, and altering fundamentally the forms of our governments;

For suspending our own legislatures, and declaring themselves invested with power to legislate for us in all cases whatsoever.

He has abdicated government here, by declaring us out of his protection and waging war against us.

He has plundered our seas, ravaged our coasts, burned our towns, and destroyed the lives of our people.

He is at this time transporting large armies of foreign mercenaries to complete the works of death, desolation and tyranny, already begun with circumstances of cruelty and perfidy scarcely paralleled in the most barbarous ages, and totally unworthy the head of a civilized nation.

He has constrained our fellow citizens taken captive on the high seas to bear arms against their country, to become the executioners of their friends and brethren, or to fall themselves by their hands.

He has excited domestic insurrections amongst us, and has endeavored to bring on the inhabitants of our frontiers, the merciless Indian savages, whose known rule of warfare, is an undistinguished destruction of all ages, sexes, and conditions.

A Statement of Independence

In every stage of these oppressions we have petitioned for redress in the most humble terms: our repeated petitions have been answered only by repeated injury. A prince, whose character is thus marked by every act which may define a tyrant is unfit to be the ruler of a free people.

Nor have we been wanting in attentions to our British brethren. We have warned them from time to time of attempts by their legislature to extend an unwarrantable jurisdiction over us. We have reminded them of the circumstances of our emigration and settlement here. We have appealed to their native justice and magnanimity, and we have conjured them by the ties of our common kindred to disavow these usurpations, which would inevitably interrupt our connections and correspondence. They too have been deaf to the voice of justice and of consanguinity.

We must, therefore, acquiesce in the necessity, which denounces our separation, and hold them, as we hold the rest of mankind, enemies in war, in peace friends.

We, therefore, the representatives of the United States of America, in General Congress, assembled, appealing to the Supreme Judge of the world for the rectitude of our intentions, do, in the name, and by the authority of the good people of these colonies, solemnly publish and declare, that these united colonies are, and of right ought to be free and independent states; that they are absolved from all allegiance to the British Crown, and that all political connection between them and the state of Great Britain, is and ought to be totally dissolved; and that as free and independent states, they have full power to levy war, conclude peace, contract alliances, establish commerce, and to do all other acts and things which independent states may of right do. And for the support of this declaration, with a firm reliance on the protection of Divine Providence, we mutually pledge to each other our lives, our fortunes, and our sacred honor.

Signed by John Hancock of Massachusetts as President of the Congress and by the fifty-five other Representatives of the thirteen United States of America:

NEW HAMPSHIRE
Josiah Bartlett
William Whipple
Matthew Thornton

MASSACHUSETTS BAY
Samuel Adams
John Adams
Robert Treat Paine
Elbridge Gerry

RHODE ISLAND
Stephen Hopkins
William Ellery

CONNECTICUT
Roger Sherman
Samuel Huntington
William Williams
Oliver Wolcott

NEW YORK
William Floyd
Philip Livingston
Francis Lewis
Lewis Morris

NEW JERSEY
Richard Stockton
John Witherspoon
Francis Hopkinson
John Hart
Abraham Clark

PENNSYLVANIA
Robert Morris
Benjamin Rush
Benjamin Franklin
John Morton
George Clymer
James Smith
George Taylor
James Wilson
George Ross

DELAWARE
Caesar Rodney
George Read
Thomas M'Kean

MARYLAND
Samuel Chase
William Paca
Thomas Stone
Charles Carroll of Carrollton

VIRGINIA
George Wythe
Richard Henry Lee
Thomas Jefferson
Benjamin Harrison
Thomas Nelson, Jr.
Francis Lightfoot Lee
Carter Braxton

NORTH CAROLINA
William Hooper
Joseph Hewes
John Penn

SOUTH CAROLINA
Edward Rutledge
Thomas Heyward, Jr.
Thomas Lynch, Jr.
Arthur Middleton

GEORGIA
Button Gwinnett
Lyman Hall
George Walton

APPENDIX B

The Constitution of the United States

Preamble

We the people of the United States, in order to form a more perfect Union, establish justice, insure domestic tranquility, provide for the common defense, promote the general welfare, and secure the blessings of liberty to ourselves and our posterity, do ordain and establish this Constitution for the United States of America.

ARTICLE I:
THE LEGISLATIVE BRANCH*

Congress*

Section 1. All legislative powers herein granted shall be vested in a Congress of the United States, which shall consist of a Senate and House of Representatives.

The House of Representatives

Section 2. (1) The House of Representatives shall be composed of members chosen every second year by the people of the several states, and the electors in each state shall have the qualifications requisite for electors of the most numerous branch of the state legislature.

(2) No person shall be a representative who shall not have attained to the age of twenty-five years, and been seven years a citizen of the United States, and who shall not, when elected, be an inhabitant of that state in which he shall be chosen.

(3) Representatives and direct taxes shall be apportioned among the several states which may be included within this Union, according to their respective numbers, [which shall be determined by adding to the whole number of free persons, including those bound to service for a term of years, and excluding Indians not taxed, three-fifths of all other persons]. The actual enumeration shall be made within three years after the first meeting of the Congress of the United States, and within every subsequent term of ten years, in such manner as they shall by law direct. The number of representatives shall not exceed one for

every thirty thousand, but each state shall have at least one representative; [and until such enumeration shall be made, the state of New Hampshire shall be entitled to choose 3, Massachusetts 8, Rhode Island and Providence Plantations 1, Connecticut 5, New York 6, New Jersey 4, Pennsylvania 8, Delaware 1, Maryland 6, Virginia 10, North Carolina 5, South Carolina 5, and Georgia 3].

(4) When vacancies happen in the representation from any state, the executive authority thereof shall issue writs of election to fill such vacancies.

(5) The House of Representatives shall choose their speaker and other officers; and shall have the sole power of impeachment.

The Senate

Section 3. (1) The Senate of the United States shall be composed of two senators from each state, [chosen by the legislature thereof,] for six years; and each senator shall have one vote.

(2) Immediately after they shall be assembled in consequence of the first election, they shall be divided as equally as may be into three classes. The seats of the senators of the first class shall be vacated at the expiration of the second year, of the second class at the expiration of the fourth year, and of the third class at the expiration of the sixth year, so that one-third may be chosen every second year; [and if vacancies happen by resignation, or otherwise, during the recess of the legislature of any state, the executive thereof may make temporary appointments until the next meeting of the legislature, which shall then fill such vacancies].

(3) No person shall be a senator who shall not have attained to the age of thirty years, and been nine years a citizen of the United States, and who shall not, when elected, be an inhabitant of that state for which he shall be chosen.

(4) The Vice President of the United States shall be president of the Senate, but shall have no vote, unless they be equally divided.

(5) The Senate shall choose their other officers, and also a president *pro tempore,* in the absence of the Vice President, or when he shall exercise the office of President of the United States.

(6) The Senate shall have the sole power to try all impeachments. When sitting for that purpose, they shall be on oath or affirmation. When the President of the United States is tried, the Chief Justice shall preside: and no person shall be convicted without the concurrence of two-thirds of the members present.

(7) Judgment in cases of impeachment shall not extend further than to removal from office, and disqualification to hold and enjoy any office of honor, trust, or profit under the United States: but the party convicted shall nevertheless be liable and subject to indictment, trial, judgment, and punishment, according to law.

Organization of Congress

Section 4. (1) The times, places, and manner of holding elections for senators and representatives, shall be prescribed in each state by the legislature thereof; but the Congress may at any time by law make or alter such regulations, [except as to the places of choosing senators].

(2) The Congress shall assemble at least once in every year, [and such meeting shall be on the first Monday in December,] unless they shall by law appoint a different day.

Rules and Procedures

Section 5. (1) Each house shall be the judge of the elections, returns and qualifications of its own members, and a majority of each shall constitute a quorum to do business; but a smaller number may adjourn from day to day, and may be authorized to compel the attendance of absent members, in such manner, and under such penalties as each house may provide.

(2) Each house may determine the rules of its proceedings, punish its members for disorderly behavior, and, with the concurrence of two-thirds, expel a member.

(3) Each house shall keep a journal of its proceedings, and from time to time publish the same, excepting such parts as may in their judgment require secrecy; and the yeas and nays of the members of either house on any question shall, at the desire of one-fifth of those present, be entered on the journal.

(4) Neither house, during the session of Congress, shall, without the consent of the other, adjourn for more than three days, nor to any other place than that in which the two houses shall be sitting.

Payment and Privileges

Section 6. (1) The senators and representatives shall receive a compensation for their services, to be ascertained by law, and paid out of the treasury of the United States. They shall in all cases, except treason, felony, and breach of the peace, be privileged from arrest during their attendance at the session of their respective houses, and in going to and returning from the same; and for any speech or debate in either house, they shall not be questioned in any other place.

(2) No senator or representative shall, during the time for which he was elected, be appointed to any civil office under the authority of the United States, which shall have been created, or the emoluments whereof shall have been increased during such time; and no person holding any office under the United States, shall be a member of either house during his continuance in office.

How a Bill Becomes a Law

Section 7. (1) All bills for raising revenue shall originate in the House of Representatives; but the Senate may propose or concur with amendments as on other bills.

(2) Every bill which shall have passed the House of Representatives and the Senate, shall, before it becomes a law, be presented to the President of the United States; if he approve he shall sign it, but if not he shall return it, with his objections to that house in which it shall have originated, who shall enter the objections at large on their journal, and proceed to reconsider it. If after such reconsideration two-thirds of that house shall agree to pass the bill, it shall be sent, together with the objections, to the other house, by which it shall likewise be reconsidered, and if approved by two-thirds of that house, it shall become a law. But in all such cases the votes of both houses shall be determined by yeas and nays, and the names of the persons voting for and against the bill shall be entered on the journal of each house respectively. If any bill shall not be returned by the President within ten days (Sundays excepted) after it shall have been presented to him, the same shall be a law, in like manner as if he had signed it, unless the Congress by their adjournment prevent its return, in which case it shall not be a law.

(3) Every order, resolution, or vote to which the concurrence of the Senate and House of Representatives may be necessary (except on a question of adjournment) shall be presented to the President of the United States; and before the same shall take effect, shall be approved by him, or being disapproved by him, shall be repassed by two-thirds of the Senate and House of Representatives, according to the rules and limitations prescribed in the case of a bill.

Powers Granted to Congress

Section 8. The Congress shall have power:

(1) To lay and collect taxes, duties, imposts, and excises, to pay the debts and provide for the common defense and general welfare of the United States; but all duties, imposts, and excises shall be uniform throughout the United States;

(2) To borrow money on the credit of the United States;

(3) To regulate commerce with foreign nations, and among the several states, and with the Indian tribes;

(4) To establish a uniform rule of naturalization, and uniform laws on the subject of bankruptcies throughout the United States;

(5) To coin money, regulate the value thereof, and of foreign coin, and fix the standard of weights and measures;

(6) To provide for the punishment of counterfeiting the securities and current coin of the United States;

(7) To establish post offices and post roads;

(8) To promote the progress of science and useful arts, by securing for limited times to authors and inventors the exclusive right to their respective writings and discoveries;

(9) To constitute tribunals inferior to the Supreme Court;

(10) To define and punish piracies and felonies committed on the high seas, and offenses against the law of nations;

(11) To declare war, grant letters of marque and reprisal, and make rules concerning captures on land and water;

(12) To raise and support armies, but no appropriation of money to that use shall be for a longer term than two years;

(13) To provide and maintain a navy;

(14) To make rules for the government and regulation of the land and naval forces;

(15) To provide for calling forth the militia to execute the laws of the Union, suppress insurrections and repel invasions;

(16) To provide for organizing, arming, and disciplining, the militia, and for governing such part of them as may be employed in in the service of the United States, reserving to the states respectively, the appointment of the officers, and the authority of training the militia according to the discipline prescribed by Congress;

(17) To exercise exclusive legislation in all cases whatsoever, over such district (not exceeding ten miles square) as may, by cession of particular states, and the acceptance of Congress, become the seat of the government of the United States, and to exercise like authority over all places purchased by the consent of the legislature of the state in which the same shall be for the erection of forts, magazines, arsenals, dockyards, and other needful buildings; —And

(18) To make all laws which shall be necessary and proper for carrying into execution the foregoing powers, and all other powers vested by this Constitution in the government of the United States, or in any department or officer thereof.

Powers Denied Congress**

Section 9. (1) The migration or importation of such persons as any of the states now existing shall think proper to admit, shall not be prohibited by the Congress prior to the year one thousand eight hundred and eight, but a tax or duty may be imposed on such importation, not exceeding ten dollars for each person.

(2) The privilege of the writ of *habeas corpus* shall not be suspended, unless when in cases of rebellion or invasion the public safety may require it.

(3) No bill of attainder or *ex post facto* law shall be passed.

(4) No capitation, [or other direct,] tax shall be laid, unless in proportion to the census or enumeration herein before directed to be taken.

(5) No tax or duty shall be laid on articles exported from any state.

(6) No preference shall be given by any regulation of commerce or revenue to the ports of one state over those of

another: nor shall vessels bound to, or from, one state, be obliged to enter, clear, or pay duties in another.

(7) No money shall be drawn from the treasury, but in consequence of appropriations made by law; and a regular statement and account of the receipts and expenditures of all public money shall be published from time to time.

(8) No title of nobility shall be granted by the United States: And no person holding any office of profit or trust under them, shall, without the consent of the Congress, accept of any present, emolument, office, or title, of any kind whatever, from any king, prince, or foreign state.

Powers Denied the States

Section 10. (1) No state shall enter into any treaty, alliance, or confederation; grant letters of marque and reprisal; coin money; emit bills of credit; make anything but gold and silver coin a tender in payment of debts; pass any bill of attainder, *ex post facto* law, or law impairing the obligation of contracts, or grant any title of nobility.

(2) No state shall, without the consent of the Congress, lay any imposts or duties on imports or exports, except what may be absolutely necessary for executing its inspection laws: and the net produce of all duties and imposts, laid by any state on imports or exports, shall be for the use of the treasury of the United States; and all such laws shall be subject to the revision and control of the Congress.

(3) No state shall, without the consent of Congress, lay any duty of tonnage, keep troops, or ships of war in time of peace, enter into any agreement or compact with another state, or with a foreign power, or engage in war, unless actually invaded, or in such imminent danger as will not admit of delay.

ARTICLE II:
THE EXECUTIVE BRANCH

The President

Section 1. (1) The executive power shall be vested in a President of the United States of America. He shall hold his office during the term of four years, and, together with the Vice President, chosen for the same term, be elected, as follows:

(2) Each state shall appoint, in such manner as the legislature thereof may direct, a number of electors, equal to the whole number of senators and representatives to which the state may be entitled in the Congress: but no senator or representative, or person holding an office of trust or profit under the United States, shall be appointed an elector.

(3) [The electors shall meet in their respective states, and vote by ballot for two persons, of whom one at least shall not be an inhabitant of the same state with themselves. And they shall make a list of all the persons voted for, and of the

number of votes for each; which list they shall sign and certify, and transmit sealed to the seat of the government of the United States, directed to the president of the Senate. The president of the Senate shall, in the presence of the Senate and House of Representatives, open all the certificates, and the votes shall then be counted. The person having the greatest number of votes shall be the President, if such number be a majority of the whole number of electors appointed; and there be more than one who have such majority, and have an equal number of votes, then the House of Representatives shall immediately choose by ballot one of them for President; and if no person have a majority, then from the five highest on the list the said House shall in like manner choose the President. But in choosing the President, the votes shall be taken by states, the representation from each state having one vote; a quorum for this purpose shall consist of a member or members from two-thirds of the states, and a majority of all the states shall be necessary to a choice. In every case, after the choice of the President, the person having the greatest number of votes of the electors shall be the Vice President. But if there should remain two or more who have equal votes, the Senate shall choose from them by ballot the Vice President.]

(4) The Congress may determine the time of choosing the electors, and the day on which they shall give their votes; which day shall be the same throughout the United States.

(5) No person except a natural-born citizen, or a citizen of the United States at the time of the adoption of this Constitution, shall be eligible to the office of President; neither shall any person be eligible to that office who shall not have attained to the age of thirty-five years, and been fourteen years a resident within the United States.

(6) In case of the removal of the President from office, or of his death, resignation, or inability to discharge the powers and duties of the said office, the same shall devolve on the Vice President, and the Congress may by law provide for the case of removal, death, or resignation or inability, both of the President and Vice President, declaring what officer shall then act as President, and such officer shall act accordingly, until the disability be removed, or a President shall be elected.

(7) The President shall, at stated times, receive for his services, a compensation, which shall neither be increased or diminished during the period for which he shall have been elected, and he shall not receive within that period any other emolument from the United States, or any of them.

(8) Before he enter on the execution of his office, he shall take the following oath or affirmation: —"I do solemnly swear (or affirm) that I will faithfully execute the Office of President of the

United States, and will to the best of my ability, preserve, protect, and defend the Constitution of the United States."

Powers of the President

Section 2. (1) The President shall be commander in chief of the Army and Navy of the United States, and of the militia of the several states, when called into the actual service of the United States; he may require the opinion, in writing, of the principal officer in each of the executive departments, upon any subject relating to the duties of their respective offices, and he shall have power to grant reprieves and pardons for offenses against the United States, except in cases of impeachment.

(2) He shall have power, by and with the advice and consent of the Senate, to make treaties, provided two-thirds of the senators present concur; and he shall nominate, and by and with the advice and consent of the Senate, shall appoint ambassadors, other public ministers and consuls, judges of the Supreme Court, and all other officers of the United States, whose appointments are not herein otherwise provided for, and which shall be established by law: but the Congress may by law vest the appointment of such inferior officers, as they think proper, in the President alone, in the courts of law, or in the heads of the departments.

(3) The President shall have power to fill up all vacancies that may happen during the recess of the Senate, by grant-ing commissions which shall expire at the end of their next session.

Duties of the President

Section 3. He shall from time to time give to the Congress information of the state of the Union, and recommend to their consideration such measures as he shall judge necessary and expedient; he may, on extraordinary occasions, convene both houses, or either of them, and in case of disagreement between them, with respect to the time of adjournment, he may adjourn them to such time as he shall think proper; he shall receive ambassadors and other public ministers; he shall take care that the laws be faithfully executed, and shall commission all the officers of the United States.

Impeachment

Section 4. The President, Vice President, and all civil officers of the United States, shall be removed from office on impeachment for, and conviction of, treason, bribery, or other high crimes and misdemeanors.

ARTICLE III:
THE JUDICIAL BRANCH

Federal Courts and Judges

Section 1. The judicial power of the United States, shall be vested in one Supreme Court, and in such inferior courts as the Congress may from time to time ordain and establish. The judges, both of the Supreme and inferior courts, shall hold their offices during good behavior, and shall, at stated times, receive for their services, a compensation, which shall not be diminished during their continuance in office.

Jurisdiction of United States Courts

Section 2. (1) The judicial power shall extend to all cases, in law and equity, arising under this Constitution, the laws of the United States, and treaties made, or which shall be made, under their authority; — to all cases affecting ambassadors, other public ministers and consuls; — to all cases of admiralty and maritime jurisdiction; — to controversies to which the United States shall be party; — to controversies between two or more states; [between a state and citizens of another state;] between citizens of different states; — between citizens of the same state claiming lands under grants of different states, and between a state, or the citizens thereof, and foreign states, [citizens or subjects].

(2) In all cases affecting ambassadors, other public ministers and consuls, and those in which a state shall be party, the Supreme Court shall have original jurisdiction. In all other cases before mentioned, the Supreme Court shall have appellate jurisdiction, both as to law and fact, with such exceptions, and under such regulations as the Congress shall make.

(3) The trial of all crimes, except in cases of impeachment, shall be by jury; and such trial shall be held in the state where the said crimes shall have been committed; but when not committed within any state, the trial shall be at such place or places as the Congress may by law have directed.

Treason

Section 3. (1) Treason against the United States, shall consist only in levying war against them, or in adhering to their enemies, giving them aid and comfort. No person shall be convicted of treason unless on the testimony of two witnesses to the same overt act, or on confession in open court.

(2) The Congress shall have power to declare the punishment of treason, but no attainder of treason shall work corruption of blood, or forfeiture except during the life of the person attainted.

ARTICLE IV:
THE STATES AND THE FEDERAL GOVERNMENT

State Acts and Records

Section 1. Full faith and credit shall be given in each state to the public acts, records, and judicial proceedings of every other state. And the Congress may by general laws prescribe the manner in which such acts, records and proceedings shall be proved, and the effect thereof.

Rights of Citizens

Section 2. (1) The citizens of each state shall be entitled to all privileges and immunities of citizens in the several states.

(2) A person charged in any state with treason, felony, or other crime, who shall flee from justice, and be found in another state, shall on demand of the executive authority of the state from which he fled, be delivered up, to be removed to the state having jurisdiction of the crime.

(3) [No person held to service or labor in one state, under the laws thereof, escaping into another, shall, in consequence of any law or regulation therein, be discharged from such service or labor, but shall be delivered up on claim of the party to whom such service or labor may be due.]

New States and Territories

Section 3. (1) New states may be admitted by the Congress into this Union; but no new state shall be formed or erected within the jurisdiction of any other state; nor any state be formed by the junction of two or more states, or parts of states, without the consent of the legislatures of the states concerned as well as of the Congress.

(2) The Congress shall have power to dispose of and make all needful rules and regulations respecting the territory or other property belonging to the United States; and nothing in this Constitution shall be so construed as to prejudice any claims of the United States, or any particular state.

Protection of States Guaranteed

Section 4. The United States shall guarantee to every state in this Union a republican form of government, and shall protect each of them against invasion; and on application of the legislature, or of the executive (when the legislature cannot be convened) against domestic violence.

ARTICLE V:
AMENDING THE CONSTITUTION

The Congress, whenever two-thirds of both houses shall deem it necessary, shall propose amendments to this Constitution, or, on the application of the legislatures of two-thirds of the several states, shall call a convention for proposing amendments, which, in either case, shall be valid to all intents and purposes, as part of this Constitution, when ratified by the legislatures of three-fourths of the several states, or by conventions in three-fourths thereof, as the one or the other mode of ratification may be proposed by the Congress; provided [that no amendment which may be made prior to the year one thousand eight hundred and eight shall in any manner affect the first and fourth clauses in the ninth section of the first article; and] that no state, without its consent, shall be deprived of its equal suffrage in the Senate.

ARTICLE VI:
GENERAL PROVISIONS

(1) All debts contracted and engagements entered into, before the adoption of this Constitution, shall be as valid against the United States under this Constitution, as under the Confederation.

(2) This Constitution, and the laws of the United States which shall be made in pursuance thereof; and all treaties made, or which shall be made, under the authority of the United States, shall be the supreme law of the land; and the judges in every state shall be bound thereby, anything in the constitution or laws of any state to the contrary notwithstanding.

(3) The senators and representatives before mentioned, and the members of the several state legislatures, and all executive and judicial officers, both of the United States and of the several states, shall be bound by oath or affirmation, to support this Constitution; but no religious test shall ever be required as a qualification to any office or public trust under the United States.

ARTICLE VII:
RATIFYING THE CONSTITUTION

The ratification of the conventions of nine states, shall be sufficient for the establishment of this Constitution between the states so ratifying the same.

Done in convention by the unanimous consent of the states present the seventeenth day of September in the year of our Lord one thousand seven hundred and eighty-seven and of the independence of the United States of America the twelfth. In witness thereof we have hereunto subscribed our names,

George Washington — President and deputy from Virginia

DELAWARE
George Read
Gunning Bedford, Jr.
John Dickinson
Richard Bassett
Jacob Broom

MARYLAND
James McHenry
Dan of St. Thomas Jenifer
Daniel Carroll

VIRGINIA
John Blair
James Madison, Jr.

NORTH CAROLINA
William Blount
Richard Dobbs Spaight
Hugh Williamson

GEORGIA
William Few
Abraham Baldwin

SOUTH CAROLINA
John Rutledge
Charles Cotesworth Pinckney
Charles Pinckney
Pierce Butler

NEW HAMPSHIRE
John Langdon
Nicholas Gilman

MASSACHUSETTS
Nathanial Gorman
Rufus King

CONNECTICUT
William Samuel Johnson
Roger Sherman

NEW YORK
Alexander Hamilton

NEW JERSEY
William Livingston
David Brearley
William Paterson
Jonathan Dayton

PENNSYLVANIA
Benjamin Franklin
Thomas Mifflin
Robert Morris
George Clymer
Thomas FitzSimons
Jared Ingersoll
James Wilson
Gouverneur Morris

*   Headings and paragraph numbers have been added to help the reader. The original Constitution has only the article and section numbers.

**   For other limitations, see amendments 1 — 10 (The Bill of Rights).

APPENDIX
C

Amendments to the Constitution
The Bill of Rights

AMENDMENT 1.
Religious and Political Freedoms (1791)

Congress shall make no law respecting an establishment of religion, or prohibiting the free exercise thereof; or abridging the freedom of speech, or of the press; or the right of the people peaceably to assemble, and to petition the government for a redress of grievances.

AMENDMENT 2.
Right to Bear Arms (1791)

A well-regulated militia, being necessary to the security of a free state, the right of the people to keep and bear arms shall not be infringed.

AMENDMENT 3.
Housing of Soldiers (1791)

No soldier shall, in time of peace be quartered in any house, without the consent of the owner, nor in time of war, but in a manner to be prescribed by law.

AMENDMENT 4.
Search and Arrest Warrants (1791)

The right of the people to be secure in their persons, houses, papers, and effects, against unreasonable searches and seizures, shall not be violated, and no warrants shall issue, but upon probable cause, supported by oath or affirmation, and particularly describing the place to be searched, and the persons or things to be seized.

AMENDMENT 5.
Rights in Criminal Cases (1791)

No person shall be held to answer for a capital, or otherwise infamous crime, unless on a presentment or indictment of a grand jury, except in cases arising in the land or naval forces, or in the militia, when in actual service in time of war or public danger; nor shall any person be subject for the same offense to be twice put in jeopardy of life or limb; nor shall be compelled in any criminal case to be a witness against himself, nor be deprived of life, liberty, or property, without due process of law; nor shall private property be taken for public use, without just compensation.

AMENDMENT 6.
Rights to a Fair Trial (1791)

In all criminal prosecutions, the accused shall enjoy the right to a speedy and public trial, by an impartial jury of the state and district wherein the crime shall have been committed, which district shall have been previously ascertained by law, and to be informed of the nature and cause of the accusation; to be confronted with the witnesses against him; to have compulsory process for obtaining witnesses in his favor, and to have the assistance of counsel for his defense.

AMENDMENT 7.
Rights in Civil Cases (1791)

In suits at common law, where the value in controversy shall exceed twenty dollars, the right of trial by jury shall be preserved, and no fact tried by a jury, shall be otherwise re-examined in any court of the United States, than according to the rules of the common law.

AMENDMENT 8.
Bails, Fines, and Punishments (1791)

Excessive bail shall not be required, nor excessive fines imposed, nor cruel and unusual punishments inflicted.

AMENDMENT 9.
Rights Retained by the People (1791)

The enumeration in the Constitution, of certain rights, shall not be construed to deny or disparage others retained by the people.

AMENDMENT 10.
Powers Retained by the States and the People (1791)

The powers not delegated to the United States by the Constitution, nor prohibited by it to the states, are reserved to the states respectively, or to the people.

Amendments 11 — 26

AMENDMENT 11.
Lawsuits Against States (1795)

The judicial power of the United States shall not be construed to extend to any suit in law or equity, commenced or prosecuted against one of the United States by citizens of another state, or by citizens or subjects of any foreign state.

AMENDMENT 12.
Election of the President and Vice President (1804)

The electors shall meet in their respective states and vote by ballot for President and Vice President, one of whom, at least, shall not be an inhabitant of the same state with themselves; they shall name in their ballots the person voted for as President, and in distinct ballots the person voted for as Vice President, and they shall make distinct lists of all persons voted for as President, and of all persons voted for as Vice President, and of the number of votes for each, which lists they shall sign and certify, and transmit sealed to the seat of the government of the United States, directed to the president of the Senate; — the president of the Senate shall, in the presence of the Senate and House of Representatives, open all the certificates and the votes shall then be counted; — the person having the greatest number of votes for President, shall be the President, if such number be a majority of the whole number of electors appointed; and if no person have such majority, then from the persons having the highest numbers not exceeding three on the list of those voted for as President, the House of Representatives shall choose immediately, by ballot, the President. But in choosing the President, the votes shall be taken by states, the representation from each state having one vote; a quorum for this purpose shall consist of a member or members from two-thirds of the states, and a majority of all the states shall be necessary to a choice. And if the House of Representatives shall not choose a President whenever the right of choice shall devolve upon them, [before the fourth day of March next following,] then the Vice President shall act as President, as in the case of the death or other constitutional disability of the President. — The person having the greatest number of votes as Vice President, shall be the Vice President, if such number be a majority of the whole number of electors appointed, and if no person have a majority, then from the two highest numbers on the list, the Senate shall choose the Vice President; a quorum for the purpose shall consist of two-thirds of the whole number of senators, and a majority of the whole number shall be necessary to a choice. But no person constitutionally ineligible to the office of President shall be eligible to that of Vice President of the United States.

AMENDMENT 13.
Abolition of Slavery (1865)

Section 1. Neither slavery nor involuntary servitude, except as a punishment for crime whereof the party shall have been duly convicted, shall exist within the United States, or any place subject to their jurisdiction.

Section 2. Congress shall have power to enforce this article by appropriate legislation.

AMENDMENT 14.
Civil Rights (1868)

Section 1. All persons born or naturalized in the United States, and subject to the jurisdiction thereof, are citizens of the United States and of the state wherein they reside. No state shall make or enforce any law which shall abridge the privileges or immunities of citizens of the United States; nor shall any state deprive any person of life, liberty, or property, without due process of law; nor deny to any person within its jurisdiction the equal protection of the laws.

Section 2. Representatives shall be apportioned among the several states according to their respective numbers, counting the whole number of persons in each state, [excluding Indians not taxed]. But when the right to vote at any election for the choice of electors for President and Vice President of the United States, representatives in Congress, the executive and judicial officers of a state, or the members of the legislature thereof, is denied to any of the male inhabitants of such state, being twenty-one years of age, and citizens of the United States, or in any way abridged, except for participation in rebellion, or other crime, the basis of representation therein shall be reduced in the proportion which the number of such male citizens shall bear to the whole number of male citizens twenty-one years of age in such state.

Section 3. No person shall be a senator or representative in Congress, or elector of President and Vice President, or hold any office, civil or military, under the United States, or under any state, who, having previously taken an oath, as a member of Congress, or as an officer of the United States, or as a member of any state legislature, or as an executive or judicial officer of any state, to support the Constitution of the United States, shall have engaged in insurrection or rebellion against the same, or given aid or comfort to the enemies thereof. But Congress may by a vote of two-thirds of each House, remove such disability.

Section 4. The validity of the public debt of the United States, authorized by law, including debts incurred for payment of pensions and bounties for services in suppressing insurrection or rebellion, shall not be questioned. But neither the United States nor any state shall assume or pay any debt or obligation incurred in aid of insurrection or rebellion against the United States, or any claim for the loss or emancipation of any slave; but all such debts, obligations, and claims shall be held illegal and void.

Section 5. The Congress shall have power to enforce, by appropriate legislation, the provisions of this article.

AMENDMENT 15.
Right to Vote (1870)

Section 1. The right of citizens of the United States to vote shall not be denied or abridged by the United States or by any state on account of race, color, or previous condition of servitude.

Section 2. The Congress shall have power to enforce this article by appropriate legislation.

AMENDMENT 16.
Income Taxes (1913)

The Congress shall have power to lay and collect taxes on incomes, from whatever source derived, without apportionment among the several states, and without regard to any census or enumeration.

AMENDMENT 17.
Direct Election of Senators (1913)

(1) The Senate of the United States shall be composed of two senators from each state, elected by the people thereof for six years; and each senator shall have one vote. The electors in each state shall have the qualifications requisite for electors of the most numerous branch of the state legislatures.

(2) When vacancies happen in the representation of any state in the Senate, the executive authority of such state shall issue writs of election to fill such vacancies: provided, that the legislature of any state may empower the executive thereof to make temporary appointments until the people fill the vacancies by election as the legislature may direct.

(3) This amendment shall not be so construed as to affect the election or term of any senator chosen before it becomes valid as part of the Constitution.

AMENDMENT 18.
Prohibition of Liquor (1919)

Section 1. After one year from the ratification of this article the manu-facture, sale, or transportation of intoxicating liquors within, the importation thereof into, or the exportation thereof from the United States and all territory subject to the jurisdiction thereof for beverage purposes is hereby prohibited.

Section 2. The Congress and the several states shall have concurrent power to enforce this article by appropriate legislation.

Section 3. This article shall be inoperative unless it shall have been ratified as an amendment to the Constitution by the legislatures of the several states, as provided in the Constitution, within seven years from the date of the submission hereof to the states by the Congress.

AMENDMENT 19.
Women's Suffrage (1920)

Section 1. The right of citizens of the United States to vote shall not be denied or abridged by the United States or by any state on account of sex.

Section 2. Congress shall have power to enforce this article by appropriate legislation.

AMENDMENT 20.
Terms of the President and Congress (1933)

Section 1. The terms of the President and Vice President shall end at noon on the 20th day of January, and the terms of senators and representatives at noon on the third day of January, of the year in

which such terms would have ended if this article had not been ratified; and the terms of their successors shall then begin.

Section 2. The Congress shall assemble at least once in every year, and such meeting shall begin at noon on the third day of January, unless they shall by law appoint a different day.

Section 3. If, at the time fixed for the beginning of the term of the President, the President elect shall have died, the Vice President elect shall become President. If a President shall not have been chosen before the time fixed for the beginning of his term, of if the President elect shall have failed to qualify, then the Vice President elect shall act as President until a President shall have qualified; and the Congress may by law provide for the case wherein neither a President elect nor a Vice President elect shall have qualified, declaring who shall then act as President, or the manner in which one who is to act shall be selected, and such person shall act accordingly until a President or Vice President shall have qualified.

Section 4. The Congress may by law provide for the case of the death of any of the persons from whom the House of Representatives may choose a President whenever the right of choice shall have devolved upon them, and for the case of the death of any of the persons from whom the Senate may choose a Vice President whenever the right of choice shall have devolved upon them.

Section 5. Sections 1 and 2 shall take effect on the 15th day of October following the ratification of this article.

Section 6. This article shall be inoperative unless it shall have been ratified as an amendment to the Constitution by the legislatures of three-fourths of the several states within seven years from the date of its submission.

AMENDMENT 21.
Repeal of Prohibition (1933)

Section 1. The eighteenth article of amendment to the Constitution of the United States is hereby repealed.

Section 2. The transportation or importation into any state, territory, or possession of the United States for delivery or use therein of intoxicating liquors, in violation of the laws thereof, is hereby prohibited.

Section 3. This article shall be inoperative unless it shall have been ratified as an amendment to the Constitution by conventions in the several states, as provided in the Constitution, within seven years from the date of the submission hereof to the states by the Congress.

AMENDMENT 22.
Limitation on Presidential Terms (1951)

Section 1. No person shall be elected to the office of the President more than twice, and no person who has held the office of President, or acted as President, for more than two years of a term to which some other person was elected

President shall be elected to the office of the President more than once. But this article shall not apply to any person holding the office of President when this article was proposed by the Congress, and shall not prevent any person who may be holding the office of President, or acting as President, during the term within which this article becomes operative from holding the office of President or acting as President during the remainder of such term.

Section 2. This article shall be inoperative unless it shall have been ratified as an amendment to the Constitution by the legislatures of three-fourths of the several states within seven years from the day of its submission to the states by the Congress.

AMENDMENT 23.
Suffrage in the District of Columbia (1961)

Section 1. The district constituting the seat of government of the United States shall appoint in such manner as the Congress may direct: A number of electors of President and Vice President equal to the whole number of senators and representatives in Congress to which the district would be entitled if it were a state, but in no event more than the least populous state; they shall be in addition to those appointed by the states, but they shall be considered, for the purposes of the election of President and Vice President, to be electors appointed by a state; and they shall meet in the district and perform such duties as provided by the twelfth article of amendment.

Section 2. The Congress shall have power to enforce this article by appropriate legislation.

AMENDMENT 24.
Poll Taxes (1964)

Section 1. The right of citizens of the United States to vote in any primary or other election for President or Vice President, for electors for President or Vice President, or for senator or representative in Congress, shall not be denied or abridged by the United States or any state by reason of failure to pay any poll tax or other tax.

Section 2. The Congress shall have power to enforce this article by appropriate legislation.

AMENDMENT 25.
Presidential Disability and Succession (1967)

Section 1. In case of the removal of the President from office or of his death or resignation, the Vice President shall become President.

Section 2. Whenever there is a vacancy in the office of the Vice President, the President shall nominate a Vice President who shall take office upon confirmation by a majority vote of both houses of Congress.

Section 3. Whenever the President transmits to the president *pro tempore* of the Senate and the speaker of the House of Representatives his written declaration that he is unable to discharge the powers and duties of his office, and until he transmits to them a written declaration to the contrary, such powers and duties shall be discharged by the Vice President as acting President.

Section 4. Whenever the Vice President and a majority of either the principal officers of the executive departments or of such other body as Congress may by law provide, transmit to the president pro tempore of the Senate and the Speaker of the House of Representatives their written declaration that the President is unable to discharge the powers and duties of his office, the Vice President shall immediately assume the powers and duties of the office as acting President.

Thereafter, when the President transmits to the president pro tempore of the Senate and the speaker of the House of Representatives his written declaration that no inability exists, he shall resume the powers and duties of his office unless the Vice President and a majority of either the principal officers of the executive department or of such other body as Congress may by law provide, transmit within four days to the president pro tempore of the Senate and the Speaker of the House of Representatives their written declaration that the President is unable to discharge the powers and duties of his office. Thereupon Congress shall decide the issue, assembling with in forty-eight hours for that purpose if not in session. If the Congress, within twenty-one days after receipt of the latter written declaration, or, if Congress is not in session, within twenty-one days after Congress is required to assemble, determines by two-thirds vote of both houses that the President is unable to discharge the powers and duties of his office, the Vice President shall continue to discharge the same as acting President; otherwise, the President shall resume the powers and duties of his office.

AMENDMENT 26.
Suffrage for 18-Year-Olds (1971)

Section 1. The right of citizens of the United States, who are eighteen years of age or older, to vote shall not be denied or abridged by the United States or by any state on account of age.

Section 2. The Congress shall have power to enforce this article by appropriate legislation.

A

Accomplishments — Tasks or achievements completed.

Accused — Blamed; charged with an offense or crime.

Acquitted—Cleared from charges made.

Adjourn — To bring a meeting to an end.

Admit — To allow or permit to enter.

Admitted — Allowed to enter. (Alaska was admitted as a state in 1959.)

Adopt—To take and make as one's own.

Adviser — A person who gives information, advice, or help.

Aeronautics—The science of designing, building, and flying aircraft.

Agency — A division within the executive branch that serves a special purpose.

Allegiance — Loyalty to a cause or a country.

Ambassador — A person appointed by the president to represent the United States in a foreign country.

Ancient — Of times long past; belonging to early history.

Appeal — A request for help; in law, to ask a higher court for help.

Appoint — To name or choose a person for an office, but not by election.

Apportion—To divide and assign something according to a plan.

Article — One of the parts of a written document.

Assemble—To come together as a group.

Assembly — A group of persons gathered together, usually for a special purpose.

Authority — The power or right to command or make final decisions.

B

Balance — To keep equal in power and influence.

Ballot — The act or method of voting, or the piece of paper on which a vote is marked.

Bankrupt — Without money; legally unable to pay one's bills; ruined.

Barrier—Something that blocks the way.

Bill — A proposed new law.

Borough — A small community that governs itself, usually smaller than a town.

Boundary — Edge or dividing line marking the place where a state or other region ends.

British — Having to do with the country of Great Britain.

Budget — A plan that lists the amount of money to be taken in and the ways the money is to be spent.

C

Campaign — All the activities that a candidate takes part in, hoping to be elected; includes public appearances, speeches, and ads.

Candidate — A person who hopes to be elected to an office such as the presidency.

Capable — Having ability; skilled or competent.

Ceremony — A formal act or celebration in honor of a special event.

Challenge — To question the truth or accuracy.

Circulate — To pass out or distribute widely; for example, to circulate a newspaper.

Citizen — A person given certain rights, duties, and privileges because he or she was born in, or chooses to live in, a city, state, or country.

Civil — Having to do with citizens; a civil law case does not involve a crime but deals with the rights of private citizens.

Civil rights — Rights that belong to every American citizen. These rights are listed in the Constitution.

Civil servants — Persons who work for the government, except those in the armed forces or those elected or appointed to office.

Civilian — A person not in the military or naval service.

Coastal — Along the land beside the sea.

Collective farms — Farms that are owned by the group of people who work on them. The workers share the goods.

Combination — A grouping of people, things, or ideas that are joined together for a special reason.

Commander — A person who has full control of a group.

Commerce — The buying and selling of large amounts of goods.

Communication — A message sent by radio, mail, telephone, or by other means.

Communism — A system in which the community owns all the property and individuals share goods. There is no private ownership.

Community — The people living in an area; a group of people living together with a common interest.

Complicated — Made up of conflicting parts; hard to understand.

Compromise — A settlement of differences in which each side gives up some of its demands.

Congress — Large group made up of men and women who are elected by the voters of their own states. They make laws that are needed for all the states. There are two parts of the Congress: the House of Representatives and the Senate.

Congressional Record — A publication that lists all business carried on by Congress. It is published four times each year (quarterly).

Consent — To agree; approval.

Conservation — The official care and protection of natural resources.

Conservative — Tending to oppose or resist change.

Conservative Party — One of the two major political parties in Great Britain. It usually tries to keep the old ways and is against change.

Consider — To examine or to think over carefully.

Consumers — Persons who use goods and services for their own needs.

Contract — An agreement made by two or more persons.

Controversy — An argument or debate; a public debate.

Convention — A formal meeting called for a special purpose.

Correctional — Intended to correct or to set right; to improve.

Criticisms — Judgments that find fault with something or someone.

Criticize — To find fault with.

Custom — A common practice observed by many people.

Customs — Taxes placed on goods coming into the country.

D

Debate — An argument or discussion between persons with different views.

Decision — Act of making up one's mind; judgment.

Dedicated — Devoted to; to give one's full attention to.

Defend — To protect from attack or harm.

Definite — Certain, exact, or without doubt.

Delegate — A person chosen to speak or act for another person or group.

Democratic — A form of government in which citizens take part; a way of life that treats people of all classes equally.

Deport — To send away or to expel from a country.

Dictator — A person ruling with full control, power, and authority.

Diplomat — A person appointed or named to represent his or her country in another country.

Disagreement — A quarrel; a difference of opinion.

Dishonorable — Shameful or disgraceful.

Disorderly — Disturbing public peace.

District of Columbia — An area of land given by Maryland and Virginia for the United States capital.

Document — An official paper that contains information, such as a mortgage or a will.

Domestic — Having to do with home and family life.

Donations — A gift or contribution.

E

Economy — Manner of handling money and business.

Efficient — Acting to get results with the least amount of effort or waste.

Elector — A person chosen by a political party to vote for the president and vice president.

Electoral college — Name of the group of electors from all the states.

Eligible — Meeting all the requirements for a certain position or rank, such as statehood.

Encourage — To give courage, hope, or confidence to.

Endowment — A gift given to a person or organization that provides income for that individual or group.

Entitled — Given a right or privilege.

Environment — Surroundings.

Essays — Short compositions on special subjects.

Evidence — The objects and statements gathered and used to judge a person accused of a crime.

Executive — A person or group having the power to carry out the plans and duties of a group; for example, a president.

Executive branch — The branch of the federal government that is in charge of carrying out the laws.

Express — To make known one's thoughts, ideas, or feelings; to put an idea into words.

F

Famine — A serious shortage of food that causes people to starve.

Federal — A system of government in which power is divided between a central government and state governments.

Figurehead — A person who is the leader because of his or her name or rank. That person has no real power to make decisions for the group.

Final — The very last; definite and without change.

Financial — Having to do with money.

Foreign — Belonging outside one's own country.

Free enterprise — The freedom of private business to operate without interference from the government; the freedom of a business to compete with other businesses in its own way.

Frequency — Has to do with the position or location on the air waves that radio and television stations use. Each station or channel must broadcast at its own frequency.

Fund raising — Obtaining a sum of money through special activities and events for a special purpose.

G

Generation — All people born at about the same time; the stages or steps in a family's history. For example, a grandfather, a father, and a son are three generations.

Ghetto — A section of a city where many members of a minority group live.

Grant — A gift of money for a certain purpose.

H

House of Representatives — The larger of the two houses of Congress. The number of representatives from each state is based on the population.

Humanities — Studies that deal with human thought, such as literature, history, music, and art.

I

Immigrant — A person who enters a new country in order to settle there.

Impartial — Fair; not taking sides.

Independent — Free from the control of others; not connected with a larger group. (Texas was an independent republic before it became a state.)

Indict — To accuse or charge with a crime, usually done by a grand jury.

Indirect — Not directly planned for; secondary.

Inherit — To receive something from another after he or she leaves or dies.

Innocent — Free from evil; not guilty of a crime.

Interfere — To meddle in the business of others.

Interior — Having to do with the inside; the business within the country.

Intermarriage — Marriage between two people from different groups.

Interstate — Between or connecting two or more states.

Introduce — To bring into use; to make known.

J

Judicial — Having to do with courts of law and justice.

Judicial branch — The branch of the federal government that reviews laws and makes decisions about the laws.

Jury — Group of citizens chosen in a court of law to listen to both sides in a case and to make a decision about it.

Justice — Fair and equal treatment under the law; the use of authority to uphold what is right and lawful.

Justice of the Peace — A local law official who has the power to act on minor offenses and to perform marriages.

K

Keynote — Basic idea or ruling principle; main policy.

L

Labor — Work that produces goods or services.

Labour Party — The other major political party in Great Britain. It is usually supported by the workers.

Lawsuit — A question or case that is decided in a court of law.

Legal — Allowed by law.

Legislative branch — The branch of the federal government that has the power to propose new laws that are needed for the whole country.

Legislator — A person who makes or passes laws; member of a state lawmaking body, whether serving in the Senate or in the House of Representatives.

Legislature — Lawmaking group of a country or state with power to make laws.

Liberal — Tending to have political views that favor reforms and changes to recognize the rights of people.

Limited — Restricted.

Loyal — Faithful; true to a country or an ideal.

M

Magistrate — A minor law official similar to a justice of the peace.

Majority — The greater number or part of something; more than one-half of the total.

Mandatory — Required.

Mansion — A large home; the home of a governor or other important official.

Military — Having to do with war or the armed forces.

Minimum — The smallest number or quantity possible.

Misuse — To use something wrongly or incorrectly.

Municipal — Of or relating to a city or its government.

N

National — Having to do with the whole country or nation.

Native — Belonging to a particular place, or group, by birth.

Natural resources — Raw materials given to us by nature, such as coal, water, soil, and minerals.

Naturalization — The act of giving full citizenship to a person of foreign birth.

Nobility — A social class of people known for rank, wealth, or power.

Nuclear — Having to do with energy produced from atoms.

O

Opinion — A belief or judgment of an individual or group.

P

Pardon — To release or excuse someone from paying a penalty; to free a person from jail or prison.

Parliamentary — A decision or procedure made by Parliament, the supreme legislative body of Great Britain.

Patent — An official document granting the right to make and sell an invention.

Percentage — A part of the whole assigned to profit, taxes, commission, or other division of the total.

Permanent — Lasting a long time.

Persecution — The act of punishing those who differ in origin, religion, or social outlook.

Persuade — To urge someone to do or believe something by reasoning.

Petition — A formal written document or legal paper asking for a right or benefit from someone in authority.

Pigeonhole — To put a bill aside to be studied at a later date.

Platform — A statement of ideas, policies, and beliefs of a political party.

Politburo — The leading policy-forming committee in the former Soviet Union.

Political — Having to do with government or the actions of the government.

Popular sovereignty — Rule by the people.

Popular vote — Vote of the people; each voter has an equal voice.

Power — Ability to take action; the right to decide.

Preamble — An introduction or short statement of purpose.

President pro tempore — The elected leader in some state senates.

Presidential leadership — Form of democracy which places executive authority in one elected official. The power to make laws is placed in another branch or body.

Press — Newspapers, magazines, and the people who work for them.

Principle — A basic truth, law, or ideal of behavior.

Progressive — In favor of changing the government.

Prohibition — Ban on making and selling alcoholic beverages.

Prosecute — To take legal action against another for the purpose of punishment or settlement.

Prosper — To succeed, thrive, or to gain wealth.

Public official — A person who holds an office.

Publication — Printed or published work, such as a newspaper, magazine, or book.

Q

Qualification — A skill or quality; a condition that must be met to fill a job or position.

Qualify — To meet the requirements for doing a job or task.

Quotas — A share assigned to each number.

R

Radioactive material — Material that gives off radiation that can be harmful to people.

Random — Having no particular order or pattern.

Refuge — Protection; shelter.

Refugee — A person who flees from his or her country to find refuge from harm.

Regulate — To control or direct.

Regulations — An authoritative rule that deals with details or procedures.

Regulatory agency — An agency that controls an activity according to certain rules and regulations. The agency can enforce these rules and penalize violators.

Rehabilitation — To put back in good condition; to assist an individual in recovering his or her health or physical condition.

Reject — To refuse to accept or use.

Represent — To act in place of others; to take care of the interests of other people.

Representative — A person who is a member of the House of Representatives; one who is given the power to act for others.

Requirement — Something that is needed to do other things.

Reserved — Held aside for a special reason; for example, the states reserved some power for themselves.

Resign — To give up an office or position; to quit one's office.

Responsible — Can be depended upon; able to answer for the actions of a department or agency.

Review — To look over; to examine again.

Revise — To improve; to bring up to date.

Revolt — To go against a government or a cause.

Revolution — A sudden political overthrow of a government. Some citizens' lives could be endangered.

S

Safeguards — People or things that protect ideas or property against harm or loss.

Satisfy — To convince; to fulfill certain requirements or conditions; to provide a solution for.

Scandal — Anything that leads to shame or brings dishonor upon someone.

Security — Safety and protection.

Segregation — The act of separating a group, such as a race or a class, from a larger group.

Select — To choose carefully.

Senate — The smaller of the two houses of Congress. There are one hundred members of the Senate. Each of the fifty states elects two senators.

Senator — A person who is a member of the Senate.

Seniority — Special place in a group because of longer service.

Separation — A division or parting.

Serve — To spend a period of time carrying out a duty.

Service agency — An agency that helps, serves, or assists the public.

Session — The period of time each year when Congress works.

Similar — Alike without being the same.

Social work — Work that is done to improve the health and living conditions of the poor, aged, handicapped, or ill.

Speaker of the House — The leader of the House of Representatives.

Staff — A group of people who advise or assist a chief officer or executive.

State of the Union Message — A speech given yearly by the president before both parts of Congress.

Statehood — The condition of being a state; having all the rights and benefits of belonging to the United States of America.

Stationed — Assigned to work in a certain place.

Statistics — Numerical data gathered in order to present information.

Strict — Stern; not changing.

Sue — To bring legal action against a person; to satisfy a claim or complaint.

Superintendent — A person who is in charge or who carries out a task or program.

System — A set of rules; a way of doing things.

T

Term — A period of time for carrying out a duty.

Traditionally — Following the usual way of doing things.

Treaty — An agreement between two or more countries or states about trade, peace, or other matters.

U

Unconstitutional — Not following the rules of the U.S. Constitution; not in agreement with the rules set down in the Constitution.

Unity — Oneness; being united.

Urban — Having to do with living in a city.

V

Vacant — Empty; not occupied.

Vested — Given to or placed under someone's authority.

Veteran — A person who has served in the armed forces.

Veto — The power of the president to reject a bill sent to him by Congress.

Voting district — An area where a certain number of people live and vote for their government leaders.

W

Warrant — A written legal order authorizing something, such as a search, seizure, or arrest.

Washington, D.C. — The capital city of the United States, located between Maryland and Virginia.

Welfare — Having to do with good health, happiness, and financial well-being.

Western democracy — Democratic form of government that is found in most countries of the western half of the world.

Witness — Someone who has seen or heard something; a person who is called to testify, or tell what he or she knows, in court.

Z

Zones — Areas within a city or region that are reserved for different purposes, such as businesses or homes.

Photo Credits

Chapter 1: pages 5, 9, 12, Library of Congress

Chapter 2: pages 19, 26, Library of Congress

Chapter 4: page 57, Naval Academy photograph

Chapter 5: page 64, David Valdez, the White House; page 67, Susan Biddle, the White House; page 68, Jimmy Carter Presidential Library

Chapter 6: page 80, U. S. Department of Agriculture; page 83, Baltimore Gas and Electric Company

Chapter 7: page 92, NASA photo; page 94, Peace Corps photo by Bill Strassberger

Chapter 8: page 102, Joyce C. Naltchayan, the White House; page 103, Library of Congress

Chapter 9: page 120, State of Maryland; page 124, Commonwealth of Virginia

Chapter 11: page 151, Dave Valdez, the White House; page 154 (left), Congressman William Clay house photographer, (right) Dundalk Eagle; page 156, Library of Congress

Chapter 12: page 169, The British Embassy; page 175 (both), Norm Myers

Chapter 13: page 181, Library of Congress